W9-BRI-916

DELIVER US FROM EVIL

CINDY JACOBS

Regal

From Gospel Light
Ventura, California, U.S.A.

Published by Regal Books
Gospel Light
Ventura, California, U.S.A.
Printed in the U.S.A.

Regal Books is a ministry of Gospel Light, an evangelical Christian publisher dedicated to serving the local church. We believe God's vision for Gospel Light is to provide church leaders with biblical, user-friendly materials that will help them evangelize, disciple and minister to children, youth and families.

It is our prayer that this Regal book will help you discover biblical truth for your own life and help you meet the needs of others. May God richly bless you.

For a free catalog of resources from Regal Books/Gospel Light, please call your Christian supplier or contact us at 1-800-4-GOSPEL *or* www.regalbooks.com.

Edited by Steven Lawson

Library of Congress Cataloging-in-Publication Data
Jacobs, Cindy.
    Deliver us from evil / Cindy Jacobs.
      p. cm.
    Includes bibliographical references and index.
    ISBN 0-8307-2800-7
1. Spiritual warfare. I. Title

BV4509.5 J335 2001
261.5'13—dc21   2001048478

1 2 3 4 5 6 7 8 9 10 11 12 13 14 15 / 09 08 07 06 05 04 03 02 01

Rights for publishing this book in other languages are contracted by Gospel Light Worldwide, the international nonprofit ministry of Gospel Light. Gospel Light Worldwide also provides publishing and technical assistance to international publishers dedicated to producing Sunday School and Vacation Bible School curricula and books in the languages of the world. For additional information, visit www.gospellightworldwide.org; write to Gospel Light Worldwide, P.O. Box 3875, Ventura, CA 93006; or send an e-mail to info@gospellightworldwide.org.

DEDICATION

This book is gratefully dedicated to all of my personal prayer partners.

I am alive today because of your prayers.

CONTENTS

Acknowledgments

This is one of my favorite parts of writing a book. It may be because it is one of the last things that I do after I have finished the body of the text and am on the homestretch. However, more than that, at this point my heart turns to all of those people who have stood with me during my long, sometimes lonesome journey.

Of course, the very first thank-you goes to the Lord. You are my source and strength. Thank you so much.

I am not one of those writers who just loves to write—although I like it more than I used to. As a result, writing takes a lot of discipline and talking to myself to keep going. It also takes talking to people such as my husband, Mike. He has heard me moan about this book for two years now. I am sure he will be delighted I am finished. Thank you so much, sweetheart!

To my children, who stood in the heat of the battle, yet encouraged me on, thanks from your mom. I love you so much and am proud of you. Also, to my mom, sister and other family members who stood with me—you are the best!

For the staff at Generals of Intercession, especially Polly, who helped me with the manuscript, thank you for enduring the heat with me!

To Beth Ward, thank you for cleaning my house, praying for me and keeping my life in order!

Thank you, Peter and Doris, John and Paula and others, for reading the manuscript.

Next, to the people at Regal for their courage to put this book in print—thank you! I want to express my deepest appreciation to Steven Lawson for the excellent and in-depth job of editing that he did on this book. Thanks, Steve, you made me look good! Also, thank you, Bayard Taylor, for the work you did on the theological review. I am sure you saved me from having some stones thrown my way. God bless you!

Finally, for all my prayer partners who would "rev up those prayers" when I was losing steam. For Mary, Leslyn and Beth, the girlfriends club, for helping with research, cards and chocolate. You have my undying gratitude.

And lastly, as for my part, I think I am going to throw a party! Hallelujah, I am done! Thanks, God!

FOREWORD

My generation grew up with *Casper the Friendly the Ghost* and *Bewitched*. I watched both television shows with regularity, finding them cute, comical and entertaining. Today's millennial kids have Pokemon, *Harry Potter* and *Sabrina, the Teenage Witch*. Innocent entertainment? Innocuous fantasy? A harmless way to pass a Saturday morning? Hardly! Wolves still come in sheep's clothing; Satan still comes as an angel of light.

A few in the Church have awakened to the nefarious nature of the goblins, witches and monsters that parade across our children's television screens and occupy shelf after shelf in our toy stores. But, sadly, many have not. Casper seems so cuddly, Harry Potter so huggable. What harm can come? Plenty!

As a pastor, I teach my congregation about our enemy who seeks to devour and destroy. Does this mean that a demon resides in every doll and an evil spirit in every television show or movie? No, of course not. But a growing spiritual battle is afoot. The strategic beachhead of the current invasion seems to be entertainment, particularly what amuses our children. Moreover, the demonic infiltration of our culture goes far beyond pocket monsters and teenage spells. We need to be alerted. Inoculated by the gradual, systematic infiltration of these icons of darkness, we have become the proverbial frog in the kettle, who does not know he is being cooked. We are being programmed to accept evil and do not realize it. We must know the schemes of the enemy, so we can counterattack with strategic intercession.

Cindy Jacobs is a faithful member of my church in Colorado Springs and a longtime friend. She is bold, straightforward, balanced and sensitive. When she plays reveille, we need to arise, pay attention and act. I know of no one more qualified to write this book. She is the right person to call us into this spiritual battle against the invasion of the occult in our society.

As cofounder of Generals of Intercession and author of *Possessing the Gates of the Enemy* and *The Voice of God*, she has already led tens of thousands of Christians to the frontlines of prayer. She has taught us how to hear the voice of God, how to release prophetic gifts and what it means to war in the heavenlies.

Then, a few years back, Cindy brought to us much-needed insights into the controversial subject of women in ministry in *Women of Destiny*. Her forthright and biblically based challenge caused many people to shift their paradigms, and the Church was enlightened afresh to God's plan for women *and* men.

Now, with this new book, Cindy takes on her toughest assignment yet. She shines a spotlight on what the enemy is up to in the new millennium. Not only does she talk about games, which are entry-level tools, but she exposes an array of demonic plots. Then she digs down to uncover the very principles Satan has used generation after generation to divert people away from God and toward the occult.

Many of us would like to relegate witches to Salem or believe they only live in faraway lands. We would like to ignore what is happening around us. But Cindy will not allow us to do that. She knows the danger of naivete in the Church. She realizes that when we Christians close our eyes, we risk having our congregations as well as our culture invaded by superstition, divination and other occult influences.

A few years ago, Cindy caught wind of the growing popularity of witchcraft, the New Age movement and black magic. Alarmed, she set out to discover just how far these trends stretched. What she discovered will at first shake you to the core. Yes, there could be a witch next door. Absolutely, the children in your neighborhood could be dabbling with curses and talking to spirits. Clearly, the devil has sought to sink his claws into our churches and the very fabric of our society.

However, Cindy Jacobs does not push the panic button. Rather she masterfully walks us through steps to protect ourselves, our families and our communities. She does not stop there. Cindy goes on to show how, with the power of the Holy Spirit, we can actually undermine and turn around what Satan has intended for evil.

If you have ever wondered about Casper, Pokemon or Harry Potter, then you need to read this book. If you want to take part in upending the attack of the enemy, then you should act upon what Cindy Jacobs has researched, revealed and so clearly set before us. This is not simply a research project into the activities of the devil; it is an action plan to counter what has been exposed. With this book, we have the tools to break generational curses, protect our families and uproot the evil that would seek to surround and envelop us. Cindy Jacobs's message is one of great hope—it is a declaration that we in the Church can embrace. Now let's allow God to deliver us from evil!

Dutch Sheets
Senior Pastor
Springs Harvest Fellowship
Colorado Springs, CO

INTRODUCTION

Writing this book has been the greatest spiritual challenge I have ever dealt with in my life. At times I wanted to give up, wishing someone else would pick up the task. Yet I have finally pressed on to finish the course, because I am convinced that the Body of Christ is, for the large part, uninformed about the occult.

During the time I have been researching and writing this book, there has been what could be called an occult revival. Many people in the Church do not have any idea that this is going on, and I want to let them know.

I have also written this book to make a statement in the heavenlies that we as Christians do not have to be afraid of the works of the devil. The Greater One lives in us!

Much of the information in this book has been gleaned from occult books and websites. The Lord has given me an incredible measure of grace to read this information—which I would not normally allow in my house—then sleep like a baby afterward. Praise God forevermore!

My family has become more toughened to spiritual attacks during the writing of this book. My son, Daniel, had some interesting encounters, but he stood up well. My daughter, Mary, and her husband, Tom, likewise faced some warfare. My husband, Mike, has remained solid as a rock. In fact, we have all come through very well.

In this book, I have chosen not to write about certain aspects of the occult such as cults and the spiritualism of various tribal people. This information has been fully covered in other places.

I intend for this book to be used as resource material for generations to come. Although some of the specifics—such as the games played—may change, Satan just keeps remixing his bag of tricks and the principles will remain the same.

I also intend for this book to have a practical application to your life. As you go through each chapter you will most likely find areas of the occult that you have dabbled in, such as reading a horoscope or wearing a lucky rabbit's foot. At the end of the book I have included two chapters that will lead you through steps of repentance and breaking the bondage of the occult. In chapter 9, I have provided a checklist of occult practices. You can use this list and apply it to your own life or you can make your own.

Are you ready to have your eyes opened wide? Let's begin.

PREFACE

Over the years I have been honored to be used by God to lead scores of people out of the occult. There have been New Agers, witches, Satanists and dabblers in all sorts of divination. Much of the information I have included in this book first came to me from these wonderful people who are now free in Christ.

I have used the facts, stories and insights these former occultists have given me because they will help open our eyes to what is really happening around us and better prepare us to deal with it all. However, I need to protect these people, some of whom still face serious threats from criminal occultists. Therefore, I have not used their names and sometimes I masked the details of their stories, so they cannot be recognized. While I am not able to identify these individuals, all of the information I have used has been verified by multiple sources.

CHAPTER 1

EYES WIDE OPEN

One beautiful spring day, I ran in to a local bookstore. It was one of those huge chain outlets with a coffee bar and comfortable chairs where shoppers can relax and read. That day, as usual, I headed straight for the Christian section.

As I looked up and down the aisles, I noted a sign that read "New Age." What I thought was curiosity, but later saw as the Holy Spirit, drew me to the section. The term "New Age" was not new to me. I had taught spiritual warfare seminars in which I warned against the occult, and I had counseled people out of the New Age movement, which is largely based on Eastern metaphysics.

Yet what I saw shocked me! The section was quite large. Before me was row upon row of occult books, including some on Wicca, magic and all sorts of divination. I paused in front of the tarot-card section and read the titles: *Voodoo Tarot Cards* and *Egyptian Tarot Cards*. There were dozens to choose from. I stopped counting at 17 varieties—and that was on just one shelf! On another row, I found a kit on how to cast spells, complete with its own voodoo doll. From a section actually labeled "Occult," I pulled out primers on astral (out of body) travel, the use of psychic abilities and divination.

THE OCCULT IN OUR MIDST

My head swam at the thought of so much occult material in my nice, Christian-influenced city. I live in Colorado Springs, Colorado, where there are at least 135 ministries and several megachurches. Some people call it "Wheaton West," after the long-time center of the evangelical world, Wheaton, Illinois. In the store were students, soccer moms and little kids. My neighbors! This huge selection of occult material was right at their fingertips.

My eyes opened wide. One thing I know from being an author is that bookstores do not carry a book unless it sells. This tells me that there is a good-sized market for this kind of material *in my city*.

As I walked out of the store, I was righteously indignant. Someone had to do something about this. The Body of Christ needed to know what was happening in our nation! Many have questioned Pokemon and *Harry Potter*. But do they know how much occult material is in their cities? They had to be told!

> AS I WALKED OUT OF THE STORE, I WAS RIGHTEOUSLY INDIGNANT. THE BODY OF CHRIST NEEDED TO KNOW WHAT WAS HAPPENING IN OUR NATION!

My Investigation Begins

In the midst of my fuming, I heard a quiet little voice say, "Why don't *you* do something about it?" Of course, I knew that could not be little ole me. Sure, I had written three books. In fact, my last one, *Women of Destiny,* about the role of women in the

Church, had stirred up a hornet's nest that was just dying down. Truth be told, I was not quite ready to face any more heat.

However, the strong confirmation that I was to write about the occult came when I met with Bruce and Claudia Porter at another chain bookstore in nearby Denver. Bruce had been the pastor of 17-year-old Rachel Scott, who died in the 1999 Columbine High School shooting in Littleton, Colorado. He told me the now well-known story about the gunmen who shot Rachel in the leg and then asked, "Do you believe in God?" When she replied in the affirmative, they shot her dead.

We all remember the details of Columbine all too well. Fourteen students and one teacher dead; 23 people injured. There is strong reason to believe that the Columbine shooters were exposed to violent videos, but I have often wondered if they were also influenced by the occult. They certainly appeared to have been demonized. After all, who other than a demon-possessed person could shoot someone else in the face and then talk calmly about how the brains look as they splatter on the floor? *OK, this is strong stuff, but that is why I titled this chapter "Eyes Wide Open."*

An Introduction to Wicca

As I talked with the Porters about why the two boys had killed Rachel, I asked if they would take a walk with me to the bookstore's occult section, which we easily found. It was larger than the one in Colorado Springs. Among the books we examined was a copy of Silver RavenWolf's *Teen Witch,* one of the best-sellers on the subject. Leaping off the back cover, bold black letters ask, "So you wanna be a witch?"

My heart sank as I turned the pages. RavenWolf says she was raised in a Baptist family that regularly went to church. Her first set of tarot cards was a gift from her cousin. That began a journey of a conversion *from* Christianity to Wicca, which is the practice of witchcraft.

Written in a lively style, the book states the differences between witchcraft and Christianity. RavenWolf makes witchcraft sound plausible, even exciting. I could see how it might entice young believers or someone not rock solid in his or her Christian faith.

I showed the Porters where RavenWolf writes about the nature of the Wiccan deities:

> Witches see God as both masculine and feminine, so often we call God the Lord and the Lady. Sometimes we simply say Spirit. We realize that Allah, Jesus and Buddha are all faces of the masculine side of God; however, we also give equal importance to the feminine side of God. We call this side of God the Lady. In the Christian religion, the female part of God manifests through Mary, but Mary doesn't have equal status with God.[1]

(Something very strange happened as I was writing the last paragraph of this manuscript. My computer screen started flickering and went gray, then the program I was using closed and the entire computer shut down. I stopped to pray and asked the Lord to please have the intercessors who stand with me pray harder.)

Meanwhile, as I closed the pages of *Teen Witch* that day in the bookstore, it was clinched. I knew I had to write and warn the Body of Christ about the occult invasion in the nations of the world. When I went to the counter to buy the first occult book for my new collection, I silently prayed for strength. You should have seen the look on the woman's face at the register. I mumbled something about doing research and hurried away.

The Rising Tide of the Occult

Most of us have heard of Pokemon. It is everywhere! While it is not overtly an occult tool such as tarot cards, the popular game subtly shows kids as young as four how to dabble in clairvoyance, summon spirits and get started in other occult practices. This is dangerous stuff. Even *Newsweek* ran an article titled, "Is Pokemon Evil?" Unfortunately, the subtitle concluded, "Well, probably not. But educators and parents still worry it's gone too far."[2]

The article reveals just how widely accepted the Japanese monster game has become:

> A Los Angeles disc jockey announced a phone-in contest to win tickets to the premiere of the *Pokemon* movie. Suddenly the Warner switchboard was receiving 70,000 calls a *minute*. The message got through: Pokemon is still a monster.[3]

This is just one sign that the occult is becoming mainstreamed into the American culture. It is on the Internet, in lyrics of popular songs and in our public schools. Wiccan priests now lead invocations at city council meetings, witches convene covens on college campuses that were once Christian and police departments use psychics to track down criminals.

The U.S. military now officially permits Wicca to be practiced by its members. There is a branch at the country's largest base, Fort Hood, in Killeen, Texas.[4] These witches practice what they call *white magic* and say they cast only positive spells. It is the people who practice black magic who go around casting spells of destruction. However, Scripture strictly forbids all witchcraft, whether white or black (see Deut. 18:10-12). (Read more about how witchcraft is demonically inspired in chapter 4.)

The Occult on Television
The occult has also invaded television and movie theaters. Have you looked at *TV Guide* lately? Three shows, *Buffy the Vampire*

Slayer, Charmed and *Sabrina, The Teenage Witch*, aim their demonic themes at the teen and Generation X markets. The advertisement for *Charmed* declares: "They're everywhere." In the show, the characters Prue, Piper and Phoebe face more warlocks than they can handle. It is sobering to wonder how many latchkey kids might be watching.

Thankfully, the Fox network show *Freaky Links* was canceled midway through its first season in 2001. But that series demonstrated just how far the networks will go. *Freaky Links* also had a website that gave children easy access to information about Wicca, instructions on casting spells and links to other occult sites.

By creating shows such as *Buffy,* the media has helped push the occult. Sad to say, the American media is probably the worst culprit. We have undoubtedly polluted the nations of this world through the movies and television programs we produce.

Just how much influence did the occult and those who are demonically inspired who work in the media have on instances such as the Columbine massacre and other school shootings? We will deal with some more eye-openers in chapter 3.

Who Believes in Ghosts?
One indicator that tells us how these movies, books and TV shows affect us is what is called the Worrying Poll.

Charisma News Service on November 2, 1999, reported the results of this survey that indicated many people are spooked by horror. Nearly half the population said they believe in ghosts. Even more people expressed concern about the growing popularity of movies, books and TV shows that feature the dark side of the supernatural.

The survey, taken by Scripps Howard News Service and Ohio University, goes on to state that 25 percent of the people polled in the 1980s gave credence to spirits. By the early 1990s, 39 percent thought ghosts could be real.

The new survey also revealed that 28 percent thought that modern-day witches might have mystical powers. Fifty-four percent were concerned about the effects that contemporary books and films about "monsters [such as] vampires, witches and other supernatural creatures could have on people."[5]

This is a good time for the Body of Christ to step forward to say, "Yes, the supernatural is real but you don't need to worry because the power of God is much greater. If you want to see evidence of His power, come to our church."

WHY WE NEED TO SEE

As Christians we must be willing to become knowledgeable about the widespread infiltration of the occult into our society. This needs to be a subject that we look at in a clear-sighted, informed way.

While writing this book, I searched and searched for Christian material that exposes the occult. Sadly, I found very little. Either it is not being written, is self-published or is not being carried by bookstores. No matter the reason, prayer warriors need good, reliable sources if we are to be effective watchmen on the wall.

I am not saying that no one is taking a stand against the occult invasion. Obviously, some people pray and good writing exposing Satan's tactics appears on the Internet. But we need more.

This book is just a primer to expose this arena to the light. I hope this will be like kicking over a big rock and watching the bugs crawl out.

The Fear Factor

Early on during the research for this book, one of my prayer partners and I visited bookstores in downtown Colorado

Springs. As we sat on our haunches looking at *The Vampire Book: The Encyclopedia of the Undead*, she whispered, "Cindy, don't you feel the oppression in here?" I grinned and, in a slightly amused voice, said, "Of course! It's thick, isn't it?" I bought the heavy volume and we went home.

Many people have said to me, "Cindy, aren't you afraid to have all those occult books in your house?"

While writing this book, my eyes have opened to the realization of how afraid Christians are of the occult. Very few would request a guided tour of the library of tarot cards and Wiccan texts that I have accumulated.

Truthfully, we are insulated in the Church. For the most part, we have no idea what is going on in the secular world. We are not the kind of salt-and-light people that we need to be.

Maybe one of the reasons there is so much warfare around this subject is the Body of Christ is afraid of getting cursed or having some kind of backlash that we do not want to deal with. Beloved, we are in a battle for the souls of men and of our nations. We cannot be ignorant of Satan's devices and still fight an effectual battle.

It is important to go a little further and analyze the reason we are so afraid of occult objects. Of course, I do not believe we should keep them in our homes. I will cover this in chapter 9. However, it is possible that many believers come from a lineage of superstition. This lends strength to our fear of being cursed by witches.

Superstitious Acts

Superstition has occult principles at its core, and the cultures of the United States and other nations of the world are rife with them. Have you ever heard the adages "Don't walk under an open ladder" or "Don't open an umbrella in the house"? How about "If you break a mirror, it will bring you seven years of bad luck" or "Don't let a black cat walk across your path. It is bad luck"? Most of us have heard these adages, if not actually repeated them ourselves, which proves my point.

While superstition is defined by the dictionary as an "irrational belief," when we connect it with an ungodly supernatural belief system it becomes occult superstition. This has great power and opens a door for oppression.

There are only two sources of supernatural power in this world: that which comes from God and His kingdom and that which comes from Satan's kingdom. When we give credence to what is simply an irrational belief, then it gives an opportunity for demonic powers to go into operation through that belief. One of the most common ways many societies function in occult superstition is through a belief in luck.

In the United States, we have an enormous belief in luck. What do we say to one another before we take a test? "Good luck, Joe." "Good luck, Susie." Whether we realize it or not, when we wish someone luck we give credence to a superstitious occult custom. As Christians, our lives are not governed by luck. Our destiny is in the hands of a capable and loving God who is not capricious in nature.

This belief in luck is so ingrained in our lives that it can be difficult to cleanse our thinking from giving it credit. In fact,

> WHEN WE GIVE CREDENCE TO WHAT IS SIMPLY AN IRRATIONAL BELIEF, THEN IT GIVES AN OPPORTUNITY FOR DEMONIC POWERS TO GO INTO OPERATION THROUGH THAT BELIEF.

right after I worked on this section, I was playing a game of Monopoly with my family. I caught myself rolling the dice and saying something like, "OK now, dice, I want double sixes!" All of a sudden I stopped myself and realized that I was playing into the hands of what we call in the United States "Lady Luck." Many gamblers address "her" right before they roll dice or place a bet at the races.

A Faith Leak

This background of superstition tends to cause us to have a faith leak when we get around witches or Satanists. I have seen Christians who believe God will care for all of their needs, yet fear people in the occult. It should not be this way. If anyone should be anxious and tremble, it should be the occultists, because demonic forces heavily influence and often control their lives.

Once I was sitting in a café in Buenos Aries, Argentina, with a friend. There was a witch's convention going on in the hotel where Ed Silvoso's ministry, Harvest Evangelism, was holding a seminar. The lobby was full of displays of crystal balls, tarot cards and other occult objects. My friend looked around and breathlessly murmured, "Cindy, we are sitting in a café full of witches." I looked around and started laughing, to which she shot back, "Cindy, what are you laughing about?" I grinned and whispered back, "I was just thinking that God rounded them up just for us to pray and get them born again." She just shook her head and sighed while agreeing with a cute little "turned up" corners smile.

Please do not misunderstand, I have a healthy respect for the subject of the occult and am fully aware of the power of the spirits that surround it. For years I have taught on spiritual warfare and led groups of intercessors. While I recognize the power of the occult, I also know the Word and it says, "He Who is in you is greater than he who is in the world" (1 John 4:4). I did not have to fear being in that café in Argentina. Neither did I have to fear writing this book, nor do you have to fear reading it. Keep this in mind as you read these pages. Satan is not greater than God!

Just the Beginning

It will take courage to read this book. Believe me, it took courage for me to write it. What you read might shock you. I was surprised to find out about how many vampire cults exist in the United States and that it is common knowledge among these vampire cultists that many actually drink each other's blood. On one of my trips to downtown Colorado Springs, I discovered a store with a whole case full of vampire paraphernalia. There were rings and pendants in a glass case that one could see by pushing a button that rotated the jewelry. Yes, in my nice little city we have people who are into vampirism.

> IT WILL TAKE COURAGE TO READ THIS BOOK. BELIEVE ME, IT TOOK COURAGE FOR ME TO WRITE IT.

This is the same store (not openly occult in nature) which had row after row of *Dungeons and Dragons* books, magazines and games. As I am writing this, I am pondering the thought, *I wonder what the bookstores in your city look like.* Trips like the ones I made might cause you to come home with *your* eyes wide open.

Notes

1. Silver RavenWolf, *Teen Witch* (St. Paul, MN: Llewellyn Publications, 1998), p. 10.
2. Malcolm Jones, "Is Pokemon Evil?", *Newsweek*, November 15, 1999, p. 72.
3. Ibid.

4. *Christianity Today*, July 12, 1999.

5. "'Worrying' Poll Shows Many Spooked by Horror Emphasis," *Charisma News Service*, November 2, 1999. http://www.charismanews.com (accessed November 2, 1999).

CHAPTER 2

MAGIC, GODDESSES AND SOUL HUNTING

For this book to make sense, we need to establish a rock-solid foundation based on God's Word. It is sad to say that most believers have no idea what the Bible declares in its admonitions against magic, soul hunting, astrology, soothsaying and the like. Therefore, let's first look at what the Scriptures have to say about these occult activities.

Even though some sections of this chapter may require deep thought, please do not skip over them. The information these sections contain will be a valuable reference tool now and in the future. Here, I show what God has to say about magic and what He forbids. I also give some helpful theological stuff and define a lot of terms that will help you understand the rest of the book.

EPHESUS AS AN EXAMPLE

When we look at the admonitions against magic in the Bible, we need to understand something about the worldview at the time the Bible was written. The clearest pictures of this come to us in the book of Ephesians and as we study the city of Ephesus.

"Of all ancient Graeco-Roman cities, Ephesus, the third-largest city in the Empire, was by far the most hospitable to magicians, sorcerers and charlatans of all sorts,"[1] wrote Princeton Theological Seminary Professor Bruce M. Metzger.

With so many Ephesians involved in the occult, it is not surprising that in Acts, Paul writes about how many magicians came to know Christ as their Messiah:

> Many also of those who had believed kept coming, confessing and disclosing their practices. And many of those who practiced magic brought their books together and began burning them in the sight of all; and they counted up the price of them and found it fifty thousand pieces of silver (Acts 19:18-19, NASB).

In a commentary on this passage, author and church-growth expert C. Peter Wagner estimated the value of the books burned in Ephesus:

> All together, they were worth fifty thousand pieces of Silver. Ernst Haenchen says that "a value equivalent to 50,000 days wages goes up in flames." If each piece of silver represents a day's wage, on today's U.S.A. scale of $10 an hour for eight-hour days, or $80 a day, it would total $4 million. Quite a book burning![2]

The Occult in Paul's World

The world in which Paul lived and wrote was full of idolatry, superstition and magic. The people worshiped gods and goddesses. Artemis (referred to as "Diana of the Ephesians" in Acts 19:28), with her visible manifestations, was the leading deity in Ephesus. The Ephesians built a magnificent temple in her honor, often counted as one of the seven wonders of the ancient world.

Artemis of the Ephesians

Artemis was a huntress goddess, the mother goddess, the nature (or Earth) goddess and the fertility goddess.[3] Her Egyptian counterpart was Isis. In Ephesus, many underworld goddesses, including Hekate, Selene and Ereschigal, were also part of the mix.[4] The exact connection between the various goddesses differs, depending upon the scholar, but most agree that Hekate reigned over witchcraft[5] and that Selene was goddess over the earth.[6] Ereschigal was perhaps the darkest, with one source recounting how people called upon her when they cast love spells for homosexual partners.[7]

THE PEOPLE OF PAUL'S DAY WERE EXTREMELY SUPERSTITIOUS. THEY SPENT A LOT OF TIME CASTING SPELLS, AND THEY USED MAGICAL AMULETS TO PROTECT THEMSELVES FROM EVIL SPIRITS.

As you can see, the people of Paul's day were extremely superstitious. They spent a lot of time and effort casting spells, and they used magical amulets to protect themselves from evil spirits.

The Ephesian Letters

An amulet is a type of protective occult object worn to ward off evil spirits or to supernaturally empower an individual. The Ephesians wore amulets called *Ephesia Grammata,* or Ephesian Letters. These "letters" had no relation to the biblical book of Ephesians; rather they were magical spells that could be written on amulets. The words were used in superstitious ways for protection from evil or to provide help on special occasions. For example, there is the story of an Ephesian wrestler who competed in the ancient Olympia games wearing the Ephesia Grammata on his ankles. He repeatedly defeated his Milesian opponent until the letters were discovered and removed. The Milesian athlete then easily won three matches in a row.[8]

This may sound absurd. But believe it or not, some of these spells actually have power—if they did not, people would not use them. Some amulets are simply superstitious ornaments, but others are backed by power from the demonic realm.

Word Power

As I have researched the occult, I have been amazed by the strength and power of God's Word, particularly in the book of Ephesians. Written by Paul, Ephesians shows the power of God as overpowering the power of the occult. Paul chose certain words and names to release spiritual power. Any Gentile who became a believer in Ephesus would relate to this use of words. Paul used language that showed that God's power is far greater than that of the occult.

The prayer at the beginning of Ephesians remains especially potent for us today as we begin our study of the occult. It is absolutely essential for us to understand the point Paul is so eloquently making:

And what is the *exceeding* greatness of His power toward us who believe, according to the working of His mighty power which He worked in Christ when He raised Him from the dead and seated Him at His right hand in the heavenly places, far above all principality and power and might and dominion, and *every name that is named, not only in this age but also in that which is to come* (Eph. 1:19-21, emphasis added).

I emphasize the phrase "every name that is named" because in the magical papyri (written scrolls) of that day, strings of names were invoked to strengthen a person's protection from sickness or other types of evil spirits. Paul makes an astounding declaration to the people of the age in which he lived as well as the ages to come: Christ is supreme over all and everything. We need not fear what the powers will do to us, because we have been given a name which is above all names. Jesus' name alone is supreme over all. People in Ephesus did not need to add strings of other power names to His and we do not need to do it today.

Name Power
Biola University Professor Clinton Arnold emphasizes the implications of the phrase "every name that is named." In his outstanding book *Ephesians: Power and Magic*, Arnold writes that calling of names is meaningful in exorcism and magical chants both in Judaism and paganism. So to have a name above all other names illustrates Christ's supremacy.[9] Ephesians 1:22 extends the point with a powerful statement:

And He put all things under His feet, and gave Him to be head over all things to the church.

Note the similarity and link to Psalm 110:1:

> The LORD said to my Lord, "Sit at My right hand, till I make Your enemies Your footstool."

It is my heartfelt prayer that as you study this book, you will come to realize that through Christ and His atoning blood, we have been given all *power* and authority over every name that can be named both in heaven and on Earth. We do not need to fear demonic foes. The opposite is true. They should fear us!

Hades Overpowered

Paul strengthens his case with another powerful passage in Ephesians:

> Therefore He says, "When He ascended on high, He led captivity captive, and He gave gifts to men." (Now this [expression] "He ascended," what does it mean but that He also first descended into the lower parts of the earth? He who descended is also the One who ascended far above all the heavens, that He might fill all things) (4:8-10).

Christ "led captivity captive" by first descending into the lower parts of the earth. His subsequent departure clearly shows that Christ overthrew the dominion of Hades, the underworld, or what the Old Testament calls Sheol.

The witch of En Dor (the medium whom King Saul consulted in 1 Samuel 28) consulted with the underworld spirits, or *ov* in the Hebrew. She was not simply a medium who talked to the dead, but there is a possibility that she interrelated somehow with the spirits of the underworld.

In Paul's day, these spirits of Hades had names such as "Hekate." This particular goddess of the underworld was revered and considered to have authority over "the keys to Hades." The people of Asia Minor greatly feared Hades. Gravestone inscriptions found throughout the region prove that the people of Asia Minor greatly feared Hades.[10]

Paul's Words

Many words in Ephesians were clearly drawn from the contemporary understanding of supernatural powers in the time of Paul. As I already noted, through the inspiration of the Holy Spirit Paul repeatedly uses power words to clearly state that God's might is greater than any demonic force.

I have gone into such detail because the writers of the New Testament assumed things that we sometimes miss. The culture of Paul's day was different from ours. We need to understand the full intent of Scripture, including its cultural context, to clearly see the evil threat of the occult in any generation.

Applying the Word

Many other Scriptures define magical terms. We need to know what the Bible says as we delve into areas that, at first, may appear to be benign. This will be especially true when we look into our children's games and television shows in the next chapter, "Child's Play." Many of us have been so influenced by the occult that we may find the truth hard to swallow. Some of these things, such as the television shows *Casper the Friendly Ghost* and *Bewitched*, seem so near and dear to us. As Dutch Sheets pointed out in the foreword to this book, they bring back fond childhood memories. We can only understand the insidiousness of the belief system put into our thoughts and minds through such images when we hold it up to the light of God's Word.

Magic or Magick?

I use the word "magic" throughout this book. Let me define it here. When I write about magic, I do not mean parlor tricks or pulling a rabbit out of a hat; I use the word as an umbrella term that encompasses many other occult words. In its broadest sense, magic is

> a form of communication involving the supernatural world. An attempt is made to affect the course of present and/or future events by means of ritual actions (especially ones that involve the symbolic imitation of what the practitioner wants to happen), and/or by means of formulaic recitations which describe the desired outcome and/or invoke gods, demons, or the spirits believed to be resident in natural substances.[11]

Another biblical word for magic is "enchantment."

Magic is the general term we can use for anything related to psychics, divination, Wicca, reading tarot cards, forecasting through the stars or astrology (also a form of divination), voodoo or related activities. Those who practice magic will often spell it "magick" to separate themselves from slight-of-hand magicians who perform magical tricks. However, since most modern translations of the Bible spell the word without a *k*, that is how I will spell it.

Taking Control

Magic can also be defined as an instrument of control.[12] We will look closer at this factor later, because through control magic can even enter into the Church without our being aware of it.

At this point, you may be thinking, *Well, Cindy, you mean I was practicing magic and witchcraft when I read my astrological forecast and looked up my birthday sign?* Absolutely! Later in this book, I will help you renounce and break the power of any occult practices in which you have participated.

Through the Fire

Here is one of the clearest Scripture passages where God points out what He prohibits:

> Don't let anyone among you offer a son or daughter as a sacrifice in the fire. Don't let anyone use magic or witchcraft, or try to explain the meaning of signs. Don't let anyone try to control others with magic, and don't let them be mediums or try to talk with the spirits of dead people (Deut. 18:10-11, *NCV*).

The next verse (v. 12) declares that the Lord "hates" anyone who does these things.

The reference to parents sacrificing their children sounds eerily similar to our modern practice of abortion.

> And you shall not let any of your descendants pass through the fire to Molech, nor shall you profane the name of your God: I am the LORD (Lev. 18:21).

Molech (also called Moloch) was the Canaanite god of fire to whom children were sacrificed.[13] God often warns the Israelites to avoid Molech.[14] Today, through abortion, we give our children up to the gods of our society. This is the modern-day equivalent of making a sacrifice to Molech. While it is not intentional idolatry, it certainly is self-serving. Since sacrifice releases great power, I am sure the demonic forces are pleased by abortion, considering it an act that empowers them.

Beware of Witchcraft

A person who practices witchcraft and one who practices sorcery seem to be on the same level in Scripture. I am aware that Wiccans would take great exception when I say that witchcraft deals with evil spirits, but any spirit not invoked by the Spirit of the Living God is demonic. Paul warned the Corinthians that we cannot drink from both the cup of demons and the cup of the Lord—it must be one or the other (see 1 Cor. 10:20-21).

Soothsaying and Divination

Soothsaying and divination have similar roots. Soothsaying is the act of foretelling events. Divination takes this one step farther by interpreting omens to disclose hidden knowledge. There are many divination techniques. Sometimes it is done through sacrificing an animal and looking at its liver. The women mentioned in Acts 16:16 possessed a spirit of divination. Bible commentator Finis Dake calls it a "spirit of python or Apollo" and offers some eye-opening insights: "It was believed that all who pretended to foretell events were influenced by the spirit of Apollo Pythius. A priestess in his temple was called a Pythoness."[15]

Many shows and commercials on TV feature psychics who tell people's fortunes. Have you ever wondered how they do that? Of course, some of these psychics are fakes and only want to take the caller's money. However, there is real power behind others. Demonic spirits called "familiars" know all about the families of the inquirers and feed that information to the psychic. The psychic may think that he is helping the inquirer, but he is really sucking that person into witchcraft, which, as will be clearly demonstrated in the next section, is an abomination to God.

Spirits, Spells and Mediums

Many people in the occult, including Wiccans, conjure spirits and cast spells. Deuteronomy 18 clearly forbids such occult activities and calls them "detestable" (vv. 9,12, *NIV*). The fact that a person believes he is doing white magic does not make any difference. The Bible clearly says that we are not to cast spells, white, black or any other color.

This passage in Deuteronomy also condemns mediums and consulting with the dead. A medium consorts with underworld spirits. Mediums who claim they contact the dead can also be called spiritists, or spiritualists. Such a person uses necromancy, which means he attempts to confer with the spirits of the deceased. Spiritualism today is actually a religion that often mixes Christianity and necromancy. I will write more about this later in this book.

> MEDIUMS ALLOW A SPIRIT GUIDE TO POSSESS AND CONTROL THEM, SUPPOSEDLY LETTING DEPARTED SPIRITS SPEAK THROUGH THEIR VOCAL CORDS.

Mediums allow a spirit guide to possess and control them, supposedly letting departed spirits speak through their vocal cords. People can be quite deceived by this when, in their grief after a death in the family, they attempt to talk with their departed loved ones. It is sad to say that they do not know that they are actually talking to demons that have taken control of the medium's vocal cords.

A surprising warning against dabbling in the occult practice of astrology, or stargazing, is found in Luke 12:29. At first glance, the English translation of this verse appears pretty benign: "And do not seek what you should eat or what you should drink, nor have an anxious mind." Some translations warn against a doubtful mind or worry. However, upon delving deeper into the Greek roots of these words, it appears that "anxious mind" could imply something much stronger. It can also mean an astrologer, one skilled in meteorology and one who deals with heavenly bodies.[16] When we look at the context of the passage, we find that we are being admonished that God will provide for us and our tomorrows. This passage could be paraphrased to say: Do not seek after what you should eat or drink through the use of astrologists who claim to predict your future, rather seek me, for I am your future and will take care of you.

Many Christians believe that they need God *and* their rabbit's foot or lucky penny. I believe that in the above passage from Luke, our loving heavenly Father was trying to tell us, **"I am all you need."**

SUPERSTITION

We have all heard of sports figures who are highly superstitious. Some believe that they have a lucky streak because they chew a certain gum during the game, use a particular bat or eat at a certain restaurant.

Art Modell, the owner of the Baltimore Ravens football team, wore the same pinstriped black suit and arrived at the stadium exactly 90 minutes before the start of each playoff game in 2001. His team was on the way to the Superbowl, and he figured following the same habits would bring them good luck.[17] Sports figures are not the only ones who are superstitious. When I was a child, I would make a wish and blow out my birthday candles. Perhaps you have done that, too.

Satan does not mind stringing us along for a season—he gets empowerment in our lives through our beliefs. However, there will be a payday someday for those who rely upon the power of luck. Satan is a destroyer, and he does not give a so-called blessing without a price.

Throwing a penny in a wishing well or looking for a falling star may sound innocent, but if we stop to think about it, we must ask, "Who are we wishing to?" When we believe in luck, we turn to something outside the human realm. If that is not God, then what is it? Look again at 1 Corinthians 10:20-21. We cannot drink from the cup of demons *and* the cup of the Lord. Participation in the occult at any level is sin, and Satan knows that the Bible says we will be judged for it.

Amulets and Charms

Another often-overlooked Bible passage forbids the use of amulets, phylacteries or charms.

> Woe to the women who sew magic charms on their sleeves and make veils for the heads of people of every height to hunt souls! Will you hunt the souls of My people, and keep yourselves alive? (Ezek. 13:18).

Evidently these women used charms while casting spells to steal or control the souls of people. This sounds amazing, but it can really happen. Arnold's book on the Ephesians gives an excellent description of amulets. I strongly recommend the book to anyone wanting to know more about this.

Christian Leaders as Targets

Whenever I travel to South America I hear amazing stories of voodoo priests cursing the souls of Church leaders. It happens in Nepal, too, where Charles Mendies, who runs a Christian orphanage, tells of witch doctors creating potions aimed at missionaries.[18] Do not think it does not occur in the United States. A few years back, when a well-known pastor held revival meetings in San Francisco, a group of Wiccans gathered outside the meeting hall and cast spells against him.[19]

Hunting for souls sounds so ominous, but that is exactly what voodoo priests and witch doctors do. One day I was praying for a top religious leader who seemingly had lost his senses, left his wife of many years for a younger woman and had absolutely no remorse. It is possible that witchcraft had been worked against him. I know of situations in which witches infiltrated the homes of Christian leaders and worked spells on the men of the family to get them to fall into adultery. We are not to be ignorant of Satan's devices, lest he should take advantage of us (see 2 Cor. 2:11).

> HUNTING FOR SOULS SOUNDS SO OMINOUS, BUT THAT IS EXACTLY WHAT VOODOO PRIESTS AND WITCH DOCTORS DO.

The good news is that Scripture promises us that God is against their magic charms and He will tear them from their arms (see Ezek. 13:20).

Marriage Under Attack

Many men and women wait too long to break the power of witchcraft off their spouse's life when they first are becoming emotionally entangled with each other. Once the couple has sexual intercourse or becomes deeply involved it is much harder to break the enemy's power. This is not to say that the power cannot be broken, but to truly be free usually requires prayer and fasting.

I am sure that the last passage is one of those "eyes wide open" experiences for many in the Body of Christ. Satan is attacking marriages, especially those of Christian leaders, with a ferocity unparalleled in recent years. That is why books such as Peter Wagner's *Prayer Shield*[20] are so necessary for the body of

Christ. We need to pray for our leaders so that they will not be affected by Satanists and those in black magic who curse them and hunt their souls.

To strengthen this point, in other chapters we will look at passages of the Bible that deal with occult subjects.

SAFEGUARD THE FUTURE

Congratulations for making it this far. This was not an easy chapter for me to write. However, I have a strong conviction that I am helping to safeguard future generations through exposing the darkness of magic to the light of the gospel.

Notes

1. Clinton Arnold, *Power and Magic* (Grand Rapids, MI: Baker Book House, 1992), p. 14, quoting B. M. Metzger, "St. Paul and the Magicians," *Princeton Seminary Bulletin* 38 (1944), p. 27.
2. C. Peter Wagner, *Acts of the Holy Spirit* (Ventura, CA: Regal Books, 2000), p. 479. Within the this quote, Wagner quotes Ernst Haechen, *The Acts of the Apostles: A Commentary* (Philadelphia: The Westminster Press, 1971), p. 567.
3. Ron Ledbetter, "Artemis," *Pantheon.org,* http://www.pantheon.org/mythica/articles/a/artemis.html (accessed May 17, 2001).
4. Arnold, p. 23.
5. "Hecate's Role," *Hekate.org,* http://www.hecate.org.uk/roles.htm (accessed May 17, 2001).
6. Arnold, p. 26.
7. "Charms," *University of Pennsylvania,* http://ccat.sas.upenn.edu/jod/apuleius/renberg (accessed May 22, 2001).
8. Arnold, p. 15.
9. Ibid., p. 54.
10. Ibid., p. 58.
11. J. A. Scurlock. *Magic* (ANE) in the Anchor Bible Dictionary, vol. IV (New York: Doubleday, 1992), p. 464.
12. Joanne K. Kuemmerlin-McLean, *Divination and Magic in the Religion of Ancient Israel,* "Thesis," (Nashville, TN: Vanderbilt University, 1989), p. 470, C, lb.

13. Finis Jennings Dake, *The Dake Annotated Reference Bible* (Lawrenceville, GA: Dake Publishing, 1963), p. 142.

14. The Columbia Encyclopedia, Sixth Edition. 2001, Columbia University Press, *Bartleby.com,* "Molech." http://www.bartleby.com/65/mo/ Molech.html (accessed May 29, 2001).

15. See Lev. 20:2-5; 2 Kings 23:10; Jer. 32:35.

16. Henry Liddell and Robert Scott, *A Greek-English Lexicon* (Oxford: The Clarendon Press, 1968), p. 1120.

17. Jarrett Bell, "Modell Seeks Last Hurrah," January 12, 2001. *USATODAY.com.*http://ads.usatoday.com/sports/nfl/story22.htm (accessed April 20, 2001).

18. Charles Mendies, interview by Steven Lawson, Christian Solidarity International, Washington, D.C., 1983.

19. Dave O'Brien, "Reborn Again?", *San Jose Mercury News*, December 14, 1991, n.p.

20. C. Peter Wagner, *Prayer Shield* (Ventura, CA: Regal Books, 1992).

CHAPTER 3

CHILD'S PLAY

Now that we are functioning with our eyes wide open, let's take a closer look at one of the most serious threats the current occult invasion poses to our society. While many of us have been walking around with our eyes shut, the enemy has crept into the games our children play, the movies they watch and the books they read.

We may not be aware of what is happening to our children, but we only have to turn on the news to know that something very awful is at work. We hear about low test scores, drug addiction, children suing their parents, rampant vandalism, kids shooting kids and much more. This is shocking, considering that we currently have in place one of the most powerful prayer movements in the history of the Church.

Could it be that we have underestimated the power and breadth of the occult as we have sought answers to our nation's problems? Could it be that we have not gone to the root of the problem where the enemy plants the first seeds of magic, superstition and witchcraft in our children? While today's games, books and movies will someday fall out of favor, Satan will use the same deceptive principles again and again. When we see the wicked pattern at work in a particular game, we will be able to apply what we learn to other forms of entertainment. We will also better understand the influence of some games and shows we may have enjoyed in our own childhood.

It is time we become more familiar with today's amusements.

THE GAMES OUR CHILDREN PLAY

I mentioned Pokemon in chapter 1. It is one of the most popular and most dangerous games our children play today. But it is not the only one. In fact, it is just a stepping stone to other fantasy games that lead children deeper into the occult.

The Pokemon Invasion

Satoshi Tajiri created Pokemon in 1996. He designed it for Nintendo's Game Boy, an electronic toy, and it become popular in Japan. In 1998, Nintendo, in cooperation with Hasbro's Wizards of the Coast division, introduced the game in the United States and it quickly became a hit here, too. The Yellow version sold more than 1 million copies in its first month of release.[1]

Pokemon has gone far beyond Game Boys. Today it features a trading-card game, a video game, a television show, several movies and a variety of accompanying merchandise. There is even a Pokemon website and world-championship tournament.

What Pokemon Teaches

"Pokemon" is short for "pocket monster." As of this writing, it featured more than 150 creatures. At first these made-up characters may seem to be innocuous. But a careful examination reveals troubling similarities with some Wiccan and other occult practices.

Each Pokemon has a unique set of magical powers which grow and evolve. Players, mostly children, are encouraged to carry their Pokemon with them wherever they go. According to the official tournament rules, holding Pokemon power in their hands will make them "ready for anything."[2]

The Pokemon are pictured on cards which can be purchased in sets or acquired through trading and by fighting with other Pokemon. The more powerful the Pokemon, the more difficult it is to get that card.

Players are called trainers. The more skilled the trainer, the more Pokemon he or she collects. Ash is the boy hero and model trainer. Children are supposed to strive to follow his example. In one episode of the Pokemon television show, Ash captures his fifth little Pokemon. But his mentor tells him five are not enough. Ash must catch lots more if he wants to be a Pokemon master—the more he gathers and trains, the more power he will have in future battles.

So Ash searches for more of the reclusive, power-filled little Pokemon. He must first find the psychic Pokemon called Kadabra and snatch it from its telepathic, pink-eyed trainer Sabrina. With the Pokemon ghost Haunter on his side, this should be a cinch!

But Ash underestimates the power of his opponent. When he battles Sabrina, each hurl their chosen Pokemon into the air, but only Kadabra evolves into a supermonster. Haunter hides. "Looks like your ghost Pokemon got spooked," taunts Sabrina.[3]

Another Pokemon dialogue reveals the moral values the game teaches. Ponder the influence this could have on children: "You can catch a Mew by cheating with a Gameshark."

"Ah, the Gameshark. Cheating is not honorable. But many of you have requested and sent me this information, so I have put it up for all you cheaters."[4]

Gengar, yet another made-up creature, has the power to curse Pokemon players. This teaches children that cursing through magic is OK. Pokemon further models ungodly character traits such as gambling.

This fantasy game, which clearly seduces our children, introduces them to the demonic realm. In his book *Pokemon and Harry Potter: A Fatal Attraction*, pastor Phil Arms does an excellent job of showing how Pokemon embodies New Age and occultlike characteristics. I will list just two here.

- The Pokemon Evee can be morphed, or changed, into three different kinds of Pokemon. The trainer, however, must use stones to complete the transformation. In Pokemon, there are water stones, thunder stones and fire stones. Several other Pokemon can be altered by these stones as well. "Many kinds of stones have been taught by occultists to have mediumistic capabilities. New Age proponents believe that some stones, such as crystals, can give off energy that has the ability to heal and even transmit thoughts," Arms writes.[5]
- The Pokemon Psyduck has incredible telepathy or mental powers. Too bad he thinks they are his own and does not realize it is actually demons that empower him. "Psyduck defeats his opponents by mesmerizing them with a piercing stare and releasing a barrage of pent-up mental energy. The New Age concept that parallels this ability falls under the heading of an altered state of consciousness," Arms explains.[6]

Children as young as four participate in Pokemon and its spin-offs. While the game's creators call it amusement, in reality as players gather more Pokemon they learn to be clairvoyant, summon spirits, practice mind-control and how to dabble in other magical arts. As we discussed in chapter two, Scripture strictly forbids all of this!

Kids Learn Math Skills?

Some Pokemon proponents boast that the game teaches kids math skills as they buy and sell cards. This may be true, but do we approve of Pokemon on these grounds? If we do, then we should also accept children running numbers at the horse track and selling drugs. When someone bets on a race, the bookie needs to know the odds. When someone sells drugs, he or she must calculate the weight of the product and know how to count cash payments.

Dangerous Side Effects

The fruit of this beginner's form of magic and witchcraft should frighten us all. The theme in Pokemon is "gotta catch them all." Such a goal can result in obsessive-compulsive behavior and violence.

Some schools have banned the game and cards because of the problems that accompany them. In Philadelphia, for example, four children at one middle school were arrested after they attacked classmates and stole their Pokemon cards. In Quebec, a 14-year-old student was stabbed in a fight over the game.[7]

One of the most alarming side effects of Pokemon occurred in Tokyo when about 700 school children reportedly suffered convulsions, vomited and displayed other symptoms while watching the Pokemon television cartoon. TV Tokyo imposed a health warning on future episodes.[8]

Just how much have our society's children been bewitched by this game? The first Pokemon movie earned $50.8 million in its first five days. Wizards of the Coast, the U.S. company based in Renton, Washington, that introduced the game in January 1998, claims to have sold more than 2 million $10 starter sets.[9]

The Bible warns us in 1 Timothy 4:1:

Now the Spirit expressly says that in latter times some will depart from the faith, giving heed to *deceiving spirits and doctrines of demons* (emphasis added).

The First Step to the Occult

"How close can we get to the occult and still call it 'good social interaction and imagination stretching fun for kids?'"[10] inquires pastor Brett Peterson about Pokemon.

It is an entry-level occult game. Wizards of the Coast hosts a website (www.wizards.com) that not only features Pokemon but also provides information on other even more dangerous fantasy games that they produce, including Magic: The Gathering and Dungeons and Dragons.

"Satan always begins with offering a bait," Phil Arms writes. "In this case, he offers children a fun-filled fantasy and diversion from reality. . . . However, as children enter into the Pokemon game, it is inevitable that they must participate in a role-playing world of fantasy."[11]

Magic: The Gathering

Magic: The Gathering is a much darker occult role-playing card game. An estimated 500,000 people participated in it in 1998, and more than 2 billion cards were sold.[12] Richard Garfield invented the game in 1993.

When I opened a deck, I could instantly tell the game was evil. Cards, which are divided into categories such as "creature" and "sorcery," show pictures of enchantments, spells and monsters. Here are a few examples from the starter game:

- The Coercion (sorcery) card says, "Human tenderness is simply weakness in a pretty package."
- The Ogre Warrior (creature) card says, "Assault and battery included."

- The Trained Orgg (creature) card says, "All orggs know how to kill; training teaches them what to kill."
- The Hand of Death (sorcery) card says, "The touch of death is never gentle."
- The Lava Axe (sorcery) card says, "Meant to cut through the body and burn straight to the soul."
- The Scathe Zombies (creature) card says, "Luckily for them, it doesn't take much brains to slaughter and maim."

In this game, empowerment comes with the collection of different colors of "manna." Manna is obtained from lands, forests and mountains. Red manna, for instance, gives players the power of red "spellcasters" who can crush the ground beneath their feet. To choose red manna is to choose action over debate. With its ability to call up such creatures as dragons, ogres and goblins, red manna is unsurpassed in aggression and excels at inflicting harm.[13] This reminds me of Jeremiah 8:12:

Were they ashamed when they had committed abomination? No! They were not at all ashamed, nor did they know how to blush.

In this verse God addresses Israelites who have backslidden and forgotten God, even though He provided them with heavenly foods, manna. In Magic: The Gathering, players do not blush in their lust for the most harmful power. And, ironically, the name of a biblical gift from God—"manna"—has been twisted and applied in a most devious way.

First Impressions
It is interesting how I first became acquainted with the game of Magic: The Gathering. The ministry my husband and I cofound-

ed, Generals of Intercession, was hosting a conference in Brooklyn, New York. This was during the time period when I was asking the Lord whether or not He wanted me to write this book. A woman sent me a note asking me if I had heard of Magic: The Gathering and enclosed a photocopy of one of the cards. I was appalled at the wickedness of the card.

Later, I returned to the hotel where I was staying. As I got out of the van to go inside I noticed a card sitting on the curb. To my surprise, it was a Magic card similar to the one I had seen depicted in the photocopy. This was not a coincidence, rather it was another nudge from the Holy Spirit telling me to get started with this project. God is amazing!

Dungeons and Dragons

An older fantasy or role-playing game that should not be overlooked is Dungeons and Dragons. It is extremely occult in nature. Originally called The Fantasy Game, it was created by Dave Arneson in 1970. It has been played by millions of people, translated into 12 languages and sold in 50 nations.[14] In 1997, Wizards of the Coast purchased Dungeons and Dragons, adding it to their growing fantasy-game catalog.

While Pokemon and Magic: The Gathering are card games, Dungeons and Dragons is an interactive, group storytelling experience. There are many manuals that tell players how to cast spells and interact with demons. The manufacturers unabashedly admit that the game is sorcery.[15] The Dungeons and Dragons *Monster Manual* lists titles of demons such as Jubilex, the faceless lord who is described as "the most disgusting and loathsome of all demons."

This game is to be avoided at all costs.

Vampire: The Masquerade

Vampire: The Masquerade is another more recent, fast-growing, role-playing game. Created by Scotsman Mark Rein-Hagen—

ironically a pastor's kid—it is intensely deviant. Players take on vampire names. Many abandon their birth names to more fully embrace the vampire role. They become creatures of the night, playing until the light dawns. The players dress the part, with a propensity for black.

Some players step beyond role playing to take on certain vampire characteristics in their everyday lives. Some file their teeth and join vampire clubs. These vampires have secret signs to communicate with each other. They bite each other's necks and arms until they draw blood, and they drink it. Drinking blood is often found in black magic practices such as Satanism. Leviticus 7:26-27 is very clear that eating blood is strictly forbidden.

> Moreover you shall not eat any blood in any of your dwellings, whether of bird or beast. Whoever eats any blood, that person shall be cut off from his people.

The Vampire Cult

While there have long been stories of vampires and various types of followers, the modern cult gained momentum when Martin V. Riccardo founded *The Journal of Vampirism* in 1977. It was one of the first periodicals devoted to vampires. Today, the popular appeal of the vampire is reflected in the dozens of active vampire interest organizations in the United States and England, each with its own regular publication. This does not even include fan clubs devoted to vampire television shows such as *Dark Shadows, Forever Knight* and *Buffy the Vampire Slayer*.

The Vampire Book: The Encyclopedia of the Undead[16] (which is around five inches thick) gives the history of books and films about vampires and it thoroughly discusses the fascination with vampires. Sections in the book cover death, immortality, forbidden sexuality, sexual power and surrender, intimacy, alienation, rebellion, violence and a fascination with the mysterious.[17]

Anne Rice's book and subsequent movie *Interview with a Vampire* are probably the instruments most used by Satan to expand the massive cult following of vampirism I have described.

I realize that reading this kind of material is not pleasant. Believe me, it is not fun to write about either. However, this is the reality that is hidden from many people today. Like I already pointed out about my own city of Colorado Springs, where I found vampire paraphernalia being sold: If they sell it, people are buying it because they want to be identified as vampires.

Ouija Board

There are many other occult games, including the Ouija Board. Created during the spiritualist revival of the mid-1800s, Ouija draws from age-old fortune-telling practices and mind-reading techniques. While many versions have been manufactured, Ouija was the first, and remains the most popular, modern-day talking board game. Amazingly it is the all-time second best-selling board game of any kind, after Monopoly.[18] Ouija Board players place their fingertips on a game piece (planchette), looking for it to move to letters or numbers, thus answering questions they have asked.

If you have played Ouija or any of the games mentioned here you may have picked up some demonic oppression and you will want to read chapter 9.

Instructions for Parents

How can parents teach their children about the dangers of the occult in games to which they will be exposed? Here are some guidelines.

1. Do not be ignorant of Satan's devices. Stay informed about the kinds of games that your child might be

introduced to through friends or at school. Walk through toy stores and take a look at what is on the shelves. If you have access to the Internet, get the web addresses off the game packages and check out the manufacturers.

2. Talk with your children frequently. Ask them what the newest games and toys are at school. If you want to go one step further, buy the item in question and look at it closely. Point out to your children that certain action figures look mean or angry. Hold the toy up to biblical standards. Is it demonic in nature? Does it display occult powers? Is it violent? Tell your children what Scripture says about each of these characteristics.

3. Read the Bible passages I have included in chapter two and explain what Scripture says about magic, witchcraft and the occult.

4. Check out your child's room. See if there is evidence of any involvement with the occult. If you find something, talk with your child about it. Do not accuse your child. Find out where he or she got the material. It may or may not be his or hers. I will go into more detail on this when we look at teenage occult practices.

WHAT ABOUT HARRY POTTER?

One day I opened the pages of *USA TODAY* and noted two children's books on the New York Times Bestseller List.[19] Both books, from a series called *Harry Potter*, had occult-sounding titles. I later noticed one of them, *Harry Potter and the Sorcerer's Stone*, in a prominent place in a local chain bookstore. Curious, I picked up a copy to read.

The *Harry Potter* series was written by an English woman named J. K. Rowling. It is remarkably easy to read. The seduction is potent because the story pulls on one's heartstrings. Its hero, Harry, is a 10-year old orphan boy who is really a powerful wizard. He lives a miserable existence with his cruel uncle and spoiled bully of a cousin. His life changes on his eleventh birthday when he finds out who he is and is accepted into the Hogwarts School of Witchcraft and Wizardry.

Young Potter's classes include riding a magical broomstick, creating potions, casting spells, self-transformation and other occult practices. This is all wrapped in a clever package meant to thrill the ordinary reader as he or she imagines Harry flying around on his incredible broomstick.

Innocent? If we do not know what Scripture teaches about magic, it might seem to be. It is really hard to criticize poor, downtrodden Harry who suddenly finds out that he is "a somebody"— in fact a very powerful individual who is anything but innocuous. He discovers that he can use his personal magical powers to do good or evil. This idea of personal power lies behind much of the appeal of *Harry Potter*, but it is a personal power apart from God. This is indeed a serious deception, one Scripture warns us about in 1 Timothy 4:1. We are to avoid all seducing, deceiving spirits. This is the same bald, crass appeal made by the serpent to Eve in the garden. Satan told her she could have knowledge of everything, and thus power. He fooled her into believing such power is attainable apart from God. This really is the lure of all magic.

Just Like Narnia?

As I have traveled around the country, many people have asked me, "Isn't *Harry Potter* fantasy just like the *Chronicles of Narnia* by C. S. Lewis?"

The answer is no. *Harry Potter* is clearly demonic in nature. It presents occult practices as being normative and good. By contrast, the *Narnia* series has clear boundaries between good and evil, and the ultimate point of the stories is redemption.

Some Christians argue that by reading *Harry Potter* it gives them an opportunity to point out to their children what is wrong with witches and sorcery. While some parents may be able to make such headway, I wonder if this is not a bit like going to an X-rated movie to teach someone about the depravity of pornography.

Tip of the Iceberg

Another eyes-wide-open moment came for me when I walked through the adolescent section of a bookstore. I estimated that about 70 percent of the reading material found there was occult in nature.

We really need to make this a matter of prayer in the Body of Christ. One thing we can intercede for is that good Christian writers would rise up and top anything the occult world produces. We need biblically based books that are readable and will capture the interest of adolescents.

Why are books such as *Harry Potter* so dangerous? To begin with, they are changing the basis of what we consider normative in our culture. There was a day when those who played with occult games were considered deviant—this is no longer true. These books are entry-level occult tools that

THESE BOOKS ARE ENTRY-LEVEL OCCULT TOOLS THAT INTRODUCE READERS TO SUCH THINGS AS WITCHCRAFT, SORCERY, SPELLS AND SPIRITUAL POWER APART FROM GOD.

introduce readers to such things as witchcraft, sorcery, spells and spiritual power apart from God. What begins as fantasy leads to real spells and potions. Books such as *Harry Potter* are door openers through which a person can become a practitioner of magic.

Phil Arms has strong words for what is happening to our children through the *Harry Potter* series:

> How tragic it is to witness these parents in their naivete and ignorance eagerly introduce their children to entertainment that is a deadly trap that could end up literally destroying their lives. . . . Harry Potter is much more aggressive [more than Pokemon and other games] in its seductive appeal to get children involved in witchcraft and the occult. . . . This wildly popular series is the most mind-boggling illustration of the psycho-spiritual assault which [our] children are now experiencing.[20]

Harry and Wicca

I know that a lot of well-meaning people, including some respected Christian leaders, scoff at the idea of *Harry Potter* increasing interest in witchcraft. But I have found it to be true. A 13-year-old Southern California girl is just one example. After reading *Harry Potter*, she sought out books about how to become a witch because she was "curious." Fortunately, this girl has a praying grandmother and did not follow through with Wicca, but many do.

Ten-year-old *Harry Potter* fan Gioia Bishop of Napa, California, told the *San Francisco Chronicle*: "I was eager to get to Hogwarts first because I like what they learned there and I want to be a witch."[21]

In England, the Pagan Federation has been barraged with so many inquiries about Wicca, mostly from teenage girls, that the group has appointed a youth officer whose primary responsibility is to respond to *Harry Potter* fans who want to know how to become a witch. "It [increased interest in witchcraft] is quite probably linked to things like *Harry Potter, Sabrina, the Teenage Witch* and *Buffy the Vampire Slayer*," Pagan Federation Media Officer Andy Norfolk told This is London, a British news website.[22]

Wiccans and other pagans themselves consider Harry Potter a good example for would-be witches such as Gioia, even though they point out that his sorcery does not follow all tenets of true witchcraft. "Perhaps it's silly to take a fictional boy wizard [Harry] as a role model. But in the realm of the invisible, where imagination is queen, the inspirations of fiction may be the most relevant. Peer deep into pagan roots and you'll find plenty of poets of impossible things. Why not take summoning spells more seriously?"[23] writes Dana Gerhardt, a self-described pagan and columnist for the *Mountain Astrologer* magazine.

Part of the seduction of books such as *Harry Potter* is the promotion of "good magic" as protection from "evil magic." This is nothing but a neo-pagan worldview. Let me explain: The pagan worldview sees the world as internally connected to a multitude of unseen forces or spirits. Some of these entities reside over natural habitats such as mountains, streams and meadows. Some are mischievous, others are malevolent. A few are spirits of the dead. In this scheme, there is no strict boundary between good and evil; rather, there is a constant tension between what we perceive as good and what we perceive as evil. In essence, this allows each person to define good for himself and seek protection from these gods, or forces, against what he has defined as evil.

This is totally at odds with the biblical worldview which focuses on God, the wise and good creator, who allows demonic evil in order that the greater good of voluntary worship may occur. In the pagan world, good and evil are presented as equals. There is no such balance in the Bible. God's good will eventually triumph over all evil. Satan has no chance. God's power is limitless and far above the power of any other principality or dominion. However, even Christians can be affected by the pagan worldview if we are not careful.

The Bible is very specific on God's opinion of those who teach paganism (and by logical extension, neo-paganism):

Woe to those who call evil good, and good evil; who put darkness for light and light for darkness (Isa. 5:20).

MARILYN MANSON AND COMPANY

Many wide-open portals to the realm of fantasy can be found in the entertainment industry. Pokemon and *Harry Potter* are good examples, but there is much more. A close look at music, video games and movies reveals how much Satan is at work. Not only do we find witchcraft taught, but we also see violence glamorized.

Other Christian writers have exposed the clear links to occult teachings in the songs of groups such as Black Sabbath, Metallica and so many others. Therefore, I will not go into detail about music in this book.

However, many people wonder how much influence the ghoulish music of Marilyn Manson and others has influenced our society. Some Columbine students claimed that Manson's lyrics, among other things, inspired shooters Eric Harris and Dylan Klebold.[24] While Manson voiced sympathy for the Columbine victims and their families, he also has made comments such as this one: "I take the role of Anti-Christ. I will scare

America, and rightfully so."[25] Community and local church leaders, understandably, did not want Manson to perform a concert in Denver. "We're not saying he caused Columbine, but we're saying he legitimizes and encourages this kind of behavior," said Colorado youth pastor Jason Janz.[26]

The movie industry, as I noted in the first chapter, also spreads occult ideas. Just look at the popular movies *Blair Witch Project, Book of Shadows* and *Practical Magic.* In fact, in late 2001, the movies *Witchcraft* and *Harry Potter and the Sorcerer's Stone* were scheduled to be released. Movies such as these can promote occult activities, and they can also plant seeds of violence. Did you know that actor Christian Slater appeared in a movie in which he wore a black trench coat and rigged the school gym bleachers with explosives to get even with the school's "in crowd"? Likewise, only this time in real life, the Columbine killers both wore black trench coats, and many people believe that part of their motivation for the killing was to get back at athletes and those in the "in crowd."

We must be vigilant as to what our children watch. The fact that the movies are rated does not keep under-aged kids out. The *Colorado Springs Gazette* sent an under-aged reporter to several theaters in our city to test whether or not she would be admitted to an R-rated movie. She was not denied admittance once.[27]

Curious about this, I stood in line at a theater in Colorado Springs and watched as tickets were being sold. I was close enough to hear people name the movie they wanted to see. Two obviously under-aged girls bought tickets to an R-rated movie without a blink of the cashier's eye.

Videos and Violence

You cannot walk through the video section of a store without having an eye-opening experience. Surveys conclude that, as of this writing, 90 percent of American households with children have rented or owned a video computer game.[28] Approximately one-third of the top 100 video games have violent content.[29] Many of them have occult themes.

Where does all of this wickedness ultimately take us? Let's turn back the clock to April 20, 1999, and revisit the worst-case scenario: the Columbine massacre in Littleton, Colorado. While it cannot be proven that the occult had anything to do with the shootings, there are some strong links. One of the biggest warning signs is a video game called Doom that Eric Harris and Dylan Klebold reportedly played.

According to Christian writer Bob Larson, six people who had been involved in school shootings played this game of death.[30] While not every child who plays Doom ends up in the occult, it is such a wicked game that we must be warned. Playing such games opens people up to demonic oppression.

All we have to do is read the packaging and instructions to know that the video game Doom is a death machine that opens demonic gates. The front of the box boldly states, "Thy Flesh Consumed." The Doom instructions are filled with profanity and demons. To survive, all that is needed is a killer instinct. One image from the Doom box was featured on Columbine killer Eric Harris's website.[31]

Many news commentators are looking for possible answers for the rash of school shootings. As of this writing, there have been 16 recent school shootings in the United States and one in Taber, Alberta, Canada. I am not aware of any secular commentator who has pointed to the demonic realm as a possible cause. However, after the shooting at Columbine, evangelist Billy Graham told an audience, "We have demons in our world. We saw them at Columbine High School not long ago. And the Bible tells us that the devil is a thief and a robber who has come to kill and destroy."[32]

How do nice young people grow up to become mass murderers? There is a strong correlation between these school shootings and occult video games. If we were able to look deeper, we would likely find connections to other occult influences as well. This is no longer child's play. Our young people are killing each other!

Playing violent videos games desensitizes the players to reality. In the games you shoot people and then they are alive at the start of the next game. This is not the case in real life. The boundaries separating fantasy and reality are blurred in the minds of many of the players. I believe that killing through fantasy opens players up to demonic influences over and over again.

The fact that fantasy killing erases the God-given lines that stop a person from taking lives arbitrarily is well known to the military of the United States. Again, quoting Larson:

> The psychology behind video games was not developed by the gaming industry. It was concocted by the military as a more efficient means of getting soldiers to kill despite natural inhibitions. After World War II the Pentagon became concerned that only 20 percent of soldiers sent into battle actually fired their weapons. By Vietnam, that rate had increased to 95 percent. The reason? Simulators were used to desensitize the soldiers so that shooting at humans was made to seem more "normal."[33]

I am not criticizing the military for its legitimate use of video games in training. That is very different from kids being amused through violent and demonic fantasy.

PARENTAL GUIDELINES

Parents, as you know, we cannot rely on society to police our children. We have to keep a watchful eye on where they spend their free time. Parents who drop their children off at the mall for seven or eight hours at a time might be surprised at what they are doing.

I am aware that things get really sticky when our children become teenagers, having raised two of them myself. Let me make a few suggestions. No matter if your children are now teenagers or not, you still have the right to know what they do in their room. Teenagers that have nothing to hide do not lock their room doors and act secretive. Of course, teenagers are growing up and want their privacy. This is not what I am talking about. I do not believe that teenagers should be allowed to lock their rooms while they are gone from the house. They are probably hiding something if they want to do this. As long as you are paying the bills for the house and they live in your home, you have every right to question their activities.

Here are some warning signs of troubled teens:

- Exhibiting belligerent behavior.
- An extreme change in dress. (I am not just talking about baggy pants and T-shirts. That is kids being kids.) I am referring to the wearing of black clothes, fingernail polish and lipstick. (Yes, some guys wear black lipstick, too.)
- Reading occult literature.
- Posting violent posters and material.
- Listening to occult rock groups such as Marilyn Manson and Metallica.

Some of you may not be familiar with "tough love" techniques. This is where intervention is done through drastic measures. Cassie Bernall was a young Christian who died a martyr's death at Columbine. At one time Cassie had become involved in witchcraft and the occult. Her parents applied tough love and made her tear down the posters in her room, throw away offensive CDs and dispose of videos that encouraged violence. They also made her go to church. As a result, she turned her life over to the Lord and is in heaven today.

I am aware that not all stories turn out as well when the parents intervene, but this still must not daunt you when you need to intervene. If you have a teenager at home that has these violent posters, take them down. Do it with your child present, if he or she will participate. If he or she throws a fit, which very well might happen, and if the child is over 18, give him or her the option of removing these things or moving out of the house and paying all of his or her own bills.

If you are a single parent, especially a woman, I suggest that you have someone with you in case you get a violent reaction. Teenagers who are into the occult can become violent. It is also a good idea to have people praying for you to bind the powers of darkness that are operating in your house and your child's room.

I think that it is good to be reminded at this point of the scriptural admonition:

Lest Satan should take advantage of us; for we are not ignorant of his devices (2 Cor. 2:11).

Christian author Berit Kjos has some sound advice on how we can teach our children to resist deception:

- KNOW THE TRUE GOD. When children know God as He has revealed Himself in His Word, they will recognize seductive counterfeits.
- SHUN OTHER GODS. It's tempting to believe the beckoning voices that display enticing counterfeits of all God's wonderful promises. The power is within yourself, they say. Do not listen to the lies. Instead take this sober warning to heart:

> When you come into the land which the LORD
> your God is giving you, you shall not learn to fol-
> low the abominations of those nations. There
> shall not be found among you . . . one who prac-
> tices witchcraft, or a soothsayer, or one who inter-
> prets omens, or a sorcerer, or one who conjures
> spells, or a medium, or a spiritist, or one who calls
> up the dead. For all who do these things are an
> abomination to the LORD (Deut. 18: 9-12).

All "these things" are demonstrated in the *Harry Potter*
books. These stories are every bit as spiritual as Christian
literature, but the spiritual power they promote comes
from other gods. If you treasure God's truth, may I
encourage your children not to read these books?[34]

Parents, let me urge you not to be intimidated by the
modern-day culture of tolerance. Being intolerant of evil is a
good thing, not a bad thing. Also, do not be afraid of a little persecution. We need to learn to be salt and light in the middle of a
decaying world. Salt sometimes burns when it is applied to a
wound, but it brings healing.

Also, if you are in a church with other parents of young children, consider forming a prayer group to intercede for each
other's families. In 1993, my husband Mike and I started a
covenantal fast with mission leaders Luis and Doris Bush. We
agreed to fast and pray for each other's children every Wednesday.
Years later we got together to rejoice over all of the answers to
prayer that we have seen for our children as they have each chosen to walk with the Lord. The fast continues to this day.

For those of you who are dealing with an at-risk child
involved in the behavior I have described, I recommend Linda
Mintle's excellent book *Kids Killing Kids*.

In this chapter, we have seen how games, books, television, music and videos lure children into a world of the occult and violence. Once they have participated in a role-playing game, the next step is to venture into the world of overt witchcraft. We look at that in the next chapter.

Notes

1. "Poke Power," *TIME for Kids*, November 12, 1999, *timeforkids.com*. http://www/timeforkids.com/TFK/archive/ 991112/991112_pokemon.html (accessed June 15, 2001).
2. "Pokemon Tournament Rules," *Wizards of the Coast*. http://www.wizards.com/ pokemon/Rules/Welcome.asp (accessed March 1, 2001).
3. Berit Kjos, "The Dangers of Role-Playing Games," *Kjos Ministries*, November 17, 1999. http://www.crossroad.to/text/articles/ pokemon599.html (accessed June 15, 2001).
4. Ibid.
5. Phil Arms, *Pokemon and Harry Potter: A Fatal Attraction* (Oklahoma City, OK: Hearthstone Publishing, 2000), pp. 42–43.
6. Ibid., p. 43.
7. *washingtonpost.com*. http://www.washingtonpost.com/wp-wrv/ aponline/19991210/aponline164808-000.h. (accessed December 10, 1999).
8. Sheryl WuDunn, "TV Cartoon's Flashes Send 700 Japanese Into Seizures," *New York Times*, December 18, 1997. http://archives.nytimes.com:80/ plweb-cgi/fastweb?state_id=992913680&view=site&docrank=1&numhits found=2&query=%28Pokemon%29%20AND%20%2819971201%3C%3Dp date%3C%3D19971230%29&query_rule=%28$query%29&query1=op2%3 DAND%26date1yyyy%3D1997%26date2yyyy%3D1997%26section% 3DALL%26thequery%3DPokemon%26fields%3DALL%26date1dd%3D01% 26date2dd%3D30%26fields2%3DALL%26thequery2%3D% 26date1mm%3D12%26thedbs%3Dcustom%26date2mm%3D12& query7=Pokemon&query8=using%20date%20range%20December% 2001,%201997%20to%20December%2030,%201997&docid=98327& docdb=1997arc&dbname=unify&numresults=10&sorting= BYRELEVANCE&operator=AND&TemplateName=abs_MPoff.tmpl& setCookie=1 (accessed June 15, 2001).
9. Malcom Jones, "Is Pokemon Evil?" *Newsweek*, November 15, 1999, n.p.
10. Brett Peterson, "Pokemon-Just Another Fad?" *Worthy News*. http:// www.worthynews.com/pokemon.htm (accessed March 30, 2001).
11. Arms, p. 68.
12. Bob Edwards, "Magic Game's Popularity," Morning Edition, National Public Radio, 1998.

13. *Magic: The Gathering, Starter Game Play Guide* (Renton, WA.: Wizards of the Coast), p. 39.
14. "Dungeons & Dragons FAQ," *Wizards of the Coast*, 2000. http://www.wizards.com/dnd/article4.asp?x=dnd/archive.3 (accessed June 15, 2001).
15. "Roleplaying Games," *Wizards of the Coast*, 2001. http://www.wizards.com/roleplaying/main.asp?x=welcome (accessed June 15, 2001).
16. J. Gordon Melton, *The Vampire Book: The Encyclopedia of the Undead* (Farmington Hills, MI: Visible Ink Press, 1999), p. ix.
17. Ibid., p. xvi.
18. Richard Webster, *Spirit Guides* and *Angel Guardians*, (Minneapolis, MN: Llewellyn Publications, 1998), pp. 168-169.
19. *Harry Potter and the Sorcerer's Stone* and *Harry Potter and the Chamber of Secrets* remain number one and number two respectively on the *New York Times* Children's Books Best-Seller List as of August 14, 2001. "Books: Best-Seller Lists," *The New York Times*. http://www.nytimes.com/pages/books/bestseller/index.html (accessed August 14, 2001).
20. Arms, pp. 76-77.
21. "What Readers Think About 'Goblet,'" *San Francisco Chronicle*, July 26, 2000. *SF Gate*. http://www.sfgate.com/cgi-bin/article.cgi?file=/chronicle/archive/2000/07/26/DD100272.DTL (accessed August 14, 2001).
22. "Potter Fans Turning to Witchcraft," *This is London*, September 4, 2001. http://www.thisislondon.co.uk/dynamic/news/story.html?in_review_id=306029&in_review_text_id=250010 (accessed September 4, 2001).
23. Dana Gerhardt, "Nagging the Invisible," *Beliefnet*, excerpted from Moon Teachings for October/November 2000, Mooncircles Newsletter, http://www.beliefnet.com/story/60/story_6076_2.html (accessed April 20, 2001).
24. Katherine Vogt, "Columbine Victims Protest Manson," *Yahoo!. News* (Associated Press), June 21, 2001. http://dailynews.yahoo.com/h/ap/20010615/us/manson_columbine_1.html (accessed June 21, 2001).
25. Marilyn Manson, *The Black Flame*, Vol. 6, Numbers 1-2, 5.
26. Vogt, "Columbine Victims."
27. *Colorado Springs Gazette*, n.d.
28. Bob Larson, *Extreme Evil, Kids Killing Kids* (Nashville, TN: Thomas Nelson Publishers, 1999), p. 39.
29. Ibid.
30. Ibid., p. 41.
31. *Indianapolis Star and News*, June 5, 1999.
32. Larson, p. 105.
33. Ibid., pp. 43-44.
34. Berit Kjos, "Bewitched by Harry Potter," *Kjos Ministries*, November 15, 1999. http://www.crossroad.to/text/articles/harrytext.html (accessed April 5, 2001).

CHAPTER 4

THE WITCH NEXT DOOR

What do you think of when you envision a witch? Is it someone who dresses all in black, perhaps with black fingernail polish, too? Is it a person who keeps animal parts in her refrigerator for spells? Is it the Wicked Witch of the West who rides a broom and taunts people with a devilish laugh? If any of these is your idea of a witch, think again.

Today's witches have re-imaged themselves: They would have us believe they are loveable and wholesome and that their craft is good. By using the best Madison Avenue marketing techniques, they have done an excellent job of changing the public's perception.

The infiltration and reinventing of this ancient craft can be found in many publications. Here is one example:

Part of the great interest on the parts of teens (in witchcraft) undoubtedly has to do with the lore of witches. . . . The reality is that witchcraft, or Wicca as it is increasingly known today, is a small but growing religion rooted in pagan traditions and has little in com-

mon with the witchcraft of popular lore. Wicca has
absolutely nothing to do with Satan, doing harm to
others, or any evil of any kind. There are several good
books for those would-be witches who come into your
library. The most essential is the appropriately titled
Teen Witch.[1]

What is the source for this quote? Perhaps you are guessing a
Wiccan journal. Not at all! It is from the *School Library Journal*
and was written by a senior librarian with the New York Public
Library. It is not hard to figure out that he is using a public-
school periodical to proselytize for the Wicca religion. It never
ceases to amaze me how the separation of church and state only
targets Christianity.

MAINSTREAMING WICCA

There is a plot afoot, a serious threat to the nations of this Earth.
This plot involves a sugarcoating and mainstreaming of witchcraft. It particularly grips our youth. Satan has done his work
well, while most of us Christians have been asleep. What is his
purpose? He seeks to reintroduce and reestablish the worship of
ancient gods and goddesses. This is not simply an American phe-
nomenon. From Scandinavia to Germany to Latin America,
witchcraft is taking root. Many times it is propagated under the
guise of "getting back to our roots."

One of the most dangerous threats to the first of the ten
commandments, "You shall have no other gods before Me"
(Exod. 20:3), is not black magic but what is known today as
white magic, particularly Wicca.

So just what is this Wicca and what do Wiccans believe? To
find out I made the eyes-wide-open journey that I talked about

in chapter 1. I decided to go to the source rather than read someone else's interpretation. I wanted to be fair enough to see what Wiccans write about themselves.

Before I go much deeper, I know that someone in the craft of Wicca might pick up this book out of curiosity. First, I want to say that I do not believe that witches should be killed. I would protect their right to life at all costs. There were many things done during what is called the Burning Times, or Times of Persecution, which I do not condone. Furthermore, I was very grieved as I studied the

> THERE IS A PLOT AFOOT, A SERIOUS THREAT TO THE NATIONS OF THIS EARTH. THIS PLOT INVOLVES A SUGARCOATING AND MAINSTREAMING OF WITCHCRAFT.

history of such occurrences. I am sorry that witches were burned, tortured and harmed in other unmentionable ways during another historic black mark: the Inquisition. In fact, many true Christians did not fare very well during this time either.

Putting Witches to Death

During the Burning Times and the Salem Witch Trials two Bible texts were used to justify the killing of witches. The first passage comes from Exodus 22:18: "You shall not permit a sorceress to live." This chapter of Exodus also says people who practice bestiality and people who sacrifice to other gods "must be destroyed."

The second passage is Leviticus 20:27 that prescribes the death penalty for anyone who consults with spirits of the dead: "A man or woman who is a medium or spiritist among you must be put to death. You are to stone them; their blood will be on their own heads."

Some witches who have written about these times believe that tens of thousands of women who used herbs and spells were put to death. I do not know the exact numbers, but there certainly were many deaths. I know that throughout history, along with witches, Christians have been burned at the stake, particularly during the Dark Ages.

Sorceresses or Poisoners?

Some Wiccan writers have suggested that the passage in Exodus has been mistranslated and that the earliest versions of the Bible indicated that a *poisoner* rather than a sorceress should not be permitted to live. I called upon Gary Greig, a Christian who is a Hebrew and Greek scholar, to check this in the most ancient texts. Here is what he wrote back to me via e-mail:

> The Hebrew term in Exodus 22:28 (22:17 in the Hebrew text of this passage), *mekhashefah,* is translated "sorceress." There is no way one can translate the Hebrew term "female poisoner" because then one would have to translate the term the same way in other passages in the Hebrew Bible. And one can hardly translate the same term, for example, in Daniel 2:2 as "poisoners." "Poisoners" would hardly be listed alongside magicians, enchanters and astrologers to interpret Nebuchadnezzar's dream.
>
> The translation "poisoner" is one possible translation of the Greek term that the Septuagint used to translate the Hebrew term in Exodus 22:18. The Septuagint is the Greek translation of the Hebrew Bible carried out in the second and third centuries B.C. in Alexandria, Egypt. They translated the Hebrew term with the Greek term *pharmakos,* which denotes "magician" or "poisoners."

The Greek term in the Septuagint translation of Exodus 22:18 cannot be translated "poisoners" because the original Hebrew term, *mekhashefah*, cannot be translated "poisoner" in the Hebrew Bible, as shown by examples of the Hebrew term in Daniel 2:2.

From this, it is clear that the passage in Leviticus was referring to sorceresses. But does this mean we are to put them to death today?

A Death Sentence for Witches?

Right about now any Wiccan reader is probably thinking, *Great, I knew they really wanted to kill us!* Not at all! This is an Old Testament Scripture that was given under the old covenant before Jesus Christ paid the price for all sin, including those which had required death under the Law. This is why God wrapped Himself in human flesh and came to Earth. His blood covers all sin, including sorcery. Therefore, *sorceresses are not to be put to death*; they are to repent and find salvation in Jesus. He is a God of love. As Christians, we do not want to see any witches put to death for practicing witchcraft; such an attitude would be grievously wrong. We want to see them born again.

While we can denounce the practices of witchcraft, we must be careful to love those

AS CHRISTIANS, WE DO NOT WANT TO SEE ANY WITCHES PUT TO DEATH FOR PRACTICING WITCHCRAFT; SUCH AN ATTITUDE WOULD BE GRIEVOUSLY WRONG. WE WANT TO SEE THEM BORN AGAIN.

who have been involved. Witches are people who need salvation through Christ just as much as any other sinner needs salvation.

WICCAN BELIEFS

What do Wiccans believe? How do their practices compare to the Bible? Let's go over some of the basics.

As I have studied a number of books and Internet sites about different forms of Wicca, I have come to see how diverse it is. Wiccan practice spans everything from a relatively innocent staring at the stars in awe to things much darker. There are many branches and practitioners of magic and witchcraft.

Wiccans Target Teens

I have interviewed high school students around the country and have found that the majority of those who attend public schools know about paganism. Non-Christian youth today are very eclectic in their belief systems. They have no problem throwing Christianity into the pile along with the rest of the religions as long as it does not interfere with the worship of many gods and goddesses.

In fact, in the book *Teen Witch*, author Silver RavenWolf wrote:

> You picked up this book, and you wonder, can witchcraft help me? My answer would be yes, indeed, but do not forget that any positive religion (Christianity, Judaism, Islam, Hinduism, Buddhism, et cetera) can give you the necessary support you need at this time of life. As you learn about witchcraft, you'll find that the religion of Wicca is not so different from the spiritual structures that you may have already experienced.[2]

Wiccans and Jesus

This kind of writing appeals to the heartstrings of most people who are not believers. It sounds so tolerant. Such an approach is easy to believe until we come to the place where Jesus said, "I am the way, the truth, and the life. No one comes to the Father except through Me" (John 14:6). I even read one Wiccan author who suggests that Jesus really meant "I am *a* way," rather than "*the* way."

I am astounded when someone suggests that Jesus was simply a good man and not God. If He was not who He said He was, then He was the most audacious person who ever lived. Who would want to consider Him as anything other than a liar if He was not truly the Son of God?

When learning about Wicca, it is important to know that Wiccans do not openly worship Satan. We will learn about satanists in chapter 5. But there is a strong case that the "horned god," also called the lord, is a reinvention of Satan even though they do not believe in him. One definition of the Craft (and understand, not all Wiccans subscribe to this definition) is "Witchcraft is a nature based, life-affirming religion that follows a moral code and seeks to build harmony among people, and empower the self and others."[3]

The Meaning of Wicca

Some Wiccans will suggest that "wicca" means "wise one." However, the roots of the word actually go back to *wikke,* which means "to bend or twist."

The Heartbeat of Wicca

There are many major differences between Wicca and Christianity. Wicca is not Christian and it is not a denomination, although there is now a national organization called the Covenant of the Goddesses which serves to coordinate the efforts of the Wiccan community.

During my study I found that there are a number of Wiccans who say, "I used to be a Christian." Many, if not all, seem to be somewhat angry with Christians. They consider Christianity a patriarchal society and very legalistic.

A young man named Phil who was celebrating the Summer Solstice with a Wiccan group in Southern California told a reporter who was researching an article for *Charisma* magazine that he left the Foursquare Church because they would not let him practice his psychic skills.[4] Of course, the Foursquare Church did the right thing, since the Bible clearly states that God forbids soothsaying. A former Baptist at the same meeting told the reporter that she had left the church because Christians wanted her to stop smoking and because they did not welcome single mothers. When the reporter asked the young woman about her understanding of the "blood of Jesus" covering her sins, the woman suddenly turned belligerent and stopped the interview.[5]

There are also quite a few Wiccan feminists, including two of their preeminent writers, Z Budapest and Starhawk.

I again want to interject here that not all of their accusations are false. While I cannot and do not condone the worship of false gods, we Christians need to be willing to admit it when we have been poor representatives of a loving God. We also need to be willing to accept all people in our midst, such as those who struggle with smoking and single mothers like the one the reporter encountered at the Summer Solstice celebration.

Female and Male Gods

Wiccans believe in and worship both a female and male god, the lady and her lord. They believe that the lady was created first by spirit. The lady sought a companion to share the world with her and the spirit created the lord for her mate. The lord is half human and half animal. Together, these two populated the planet. The lord, since he is master of the animal and vegetable kingdoms, has antlers on his head which look like a stag's.

In Wicca, the goddess and god created the human race, but it needed to be healed. Therefore, they created witches who would bring about healing through witchcraft. The lord and lady taught the witches how to cast spells, draw a magic circle and perform other occult practices.

As I have studied the worship of the lady, I have found that she has many faces. Among the names she is given as she is worshiped are Isis, Kali, Lilith (also Lilitu), Astarte, Tanit and Diana. It is appalling to think that these goddesses are worshiped when their roots are so demonic.

For instance, Kali is usually depicted with a necklace of human skulls. She is often shown dancing on the corpses of her lovers. Mike, my husband, and I have seen her worshiped in Nepal with animal sacrifices. She is a goddess of death.

Tanit is a Phoenician goddess. Under her reign during the third and fourth centuries, animal sacrifices decreased and increasing numbers of infants were sacrificed to her cult.

This is particularly disturbing when one considers the pro-abortion stance of many Wiccans. Although they may not physically be sacrificing babies, the spirit they worship still demands sacrifice. With at least 38 million babies who have been aborted to date in America alone, this bloodthirsty goddess has gained great empowerment.

You may have heard of Lilith from the musical tours in recent years by a number of well-known women musicians. Talk about a revival of paganism! Lilith is a figure out of Hebrew cabalistic folklore who was said to be Adam's first wife and who devoured her own children alive![6]

Artemis was the Greek name for the goddess, who also demanded human sacrifice. Surprisingly, Diana, the Roman goddess and equivalent of Artemis is one of the deities most

invoked and loved by Wiccans. I have seen the kind of evil propagated by this evil spirit myself on a trip to Ephesus. She pro-
moted prostitution as well as ungodly sacrifices. She was also
noted for her visible manifestations.

Wicca's Pagan Roots

Not long ago I was flying home from Washington, D.C. and
attempting to study a book on magic. A young man sat next to
me and sweetly asked, "Oh, are you a Wiccan? I'm an atheist
myself but I have a number of friends who are Wiccans." He went
on to say that Christianity basically is a new religion, simply an
adaptation of paganism. I have heard this kind of propaganda
before, but as has been confirmed through my studies, I have to
disagree. Christianity, rooted in Judaism, clearly stands apart
from all other world religions.

However, pagans did syncretize their beliefs with the
Church, especially in art. Depictions of pagan gods can be found
carved in wood and stone on buildings throughout Europe,
including the south doorframe of Whittlesford's Church of St.
Mary, in Cambridgeshire and the wall of the priory building of
St. Ives in Huntingdonshore, England.[7] Here, the goddess of fertility was depicted with greatly exaggerated female attributes.

Wiccan PR Campaign Launched

In recent years in America, Wicca has become more formalized,
having adopted a central belief system during the Spring
Witchmeet of 1974 in Minneapolis, Minnesota. Wiccans further
mainstreamed in 1994 when they were invited to become members of the World Parliament of Religions Conference in
Chicago. There are some today who say that Wicca is one of the
fastest growing religions in America. This could be true for certain age groups, such as youth or Gen-Xers. In fact, the
Covenant of the Goddesses has launched a public relations cam-

paign to reshape the image of witches. Across the country, religion reporters have been approached by local Wiccans wanting to give their side of the story and, for the most part, the reporters have written positive articles about Wicca and witches.[8]

Book of Shadows
In place of the Bible, Wiccans keep a personal Book of Shadows (BOS), also called a *grimoire*, wherein they hand-copy their spells, magical rules and other things, such as herbology. The BOS got its name when the witches had to have their meetings in secret.

One of the first people to keep a Book of Shadows was a man who has been called the grand old man of British witchcraft, Gerald Gardner. He lived on the Isle of Man, where he wrote two books which are the foundation for much of what Wiccans believe today. When the British repealed the Witchcraft Act of 1735 in 1951, which had forbidden occult practices, his works had an open door.

Satan or Lucifer?
Wiccans are taught that Satan is a biblical myth and a slander on the true god of light, Lucifer. One ex-Wiccan said that they liked to quote Dr. Margaret Murray and say, "The gods of the old religion become the devils of the new."[9] Murray was one of the early leaders of Wicca, along with Gardner. However, I find it quite curious that they worship a male god, Lucifer, whom the Bible clearly tells us fell from heaven because he wanted to be like God. Although Wiccans adamantly deny that Lucifer and Satan are one and the same, it seems that the god of this age has simply found people to worship him in a different form.

Reincarnation
One of the basic tenets of Wiccan is reincarnation. Many Wiccans believe if a person does bad things then he releases neg-

ative karma and will have to come back to start all over. Karma is a Sanskrit word that basically means whatever you do comes back at you.[10] When a person does bad things it is not called sinning, but having bad karma. Therefore, he needs to come back again in another life, and he will be put in a position to learn to be a better person. For example, a rich person who torments the poor might come back as a beggar.

People who follow this belief system contend they can recall their past lives through hypnosis or divination. Some people believe that they have to come back under each sign of the zodiac and master a different lesson each time.

Heaven and Hell

There is no heaven or hell in the Wiccan belief system, only Summerland. From there you are reborn to learn the lessons you need from life. One day I turned on the television to a very popular show called *Hercules*. The characters were talking about how Hercules's wife had been killed and how he had gone to see her in Summerland. (By the way, at one time Hercules was actually worshiped. There is a castle off the coast of southern Spain where the emperors came to worship him.) The horned god of death can be found in some forms of Wicca and it is the one who rules Summerland. A case can be made that on a spiritual level, Satan lies behind the horned god, although Wiccans would never recognize this.

People may not call it Summerland, but this idea that everyone goes to a better place "just on the other side" is very common today, not just among Wiccans, but in all of society.

A Witch's Brew and Other Spells

The use of herbs is a major part of the spells done by Wiccans. They use them for healing of various ailments. The kind of weird-sounding ingredients often thought of as being part of a witch's bubbling brew actually were folk names for herbs. Here are a few of the magical herbs and what they are used for:

Eggs: Healing, removing negativity and fertility
Endive: Lust and love
Garlic: Protection, healing, exorcism, lust, antitheft and relief from nightmares[11]

Other kinds of magic include color magic, which works when the vibrations of different colors affect the body. Here are some colors and the way they are used in magic:

Black: Returning to sender, divination, negative work and protection
Dark purple: Calling up the power of the ancient ones; sigils/runes (a type of divination from the magical alphabet)
Mint green: Gaining money (used with gold and/or silver)[12]

Some witches will only wear the color silver, because they believe that gold is a Christian metal and not for them. This does not mean that Christians need to overreact and not wear silver. It is a metal created by God. We can wear any color. We should not be restrictive just because witches or anyone else identifies with a certain color.

The Power of Spells

Witches use spells or charms to stop bleeding, sickness, disease and things like warts. Author Chuck Pierce tells the story of his visit to a witch when he was around 18. She spoke some words over the warts and moles on his arm, and they all disappeared. There is real power here, but it is based in the occult. He remembered this incident many years later when he was in a time of great spiritual warfare and realized this incident was an open door to demonic attack in his life. He renounced what he had done and thus, through the power of the blood of Jesus, closed the door to the enemy.

Hex Signs

One form of healing magic that is growing in popularity is called Powwow magic, also known as hexcraft. This is prevalent in Pennsylvania and is thought to have come over from the Black Forest area of Germany. Pennsylvania, according to witchcraft writers, was most likely an entry point for European witchcraft into the United States, where it mixed with Indian magic. The state of Pennsylvania is still thought of as Avalon or witch haven for the craft.

Witchcraft became a part of what are known today as the Pennsylvania Dutch communities. However, these people were not Dutch at all. "Dutch" was originally "Deutschland," taken from the German word for "Germany." It is true that many people in the Pennsylvania Dutch community love Jesus. Powwow magic and these hex signs are clear examples of how some Christians have ended up, often inadvertently, allowing elements of the occult into their lives.

The effects of Powwow magic worked its way into the Amish traditions, particularly with the use of hex signs. In some areas of Pennsylvania you can still see these artistic symbols posted on barns and in some homes. Originally they were meant to bring the landowner good luck or a bountiful crop. Some people contend these signs are nothing more than folk art, but they were clearly used to appease the spirits and ward off evil in the same way gargoyles have been carved in stone at some European cathedrals.

Today hex signs have become collector's items sold in country stores in Pennsylvania and on the internet. If you have ever brought one home, you should destroy it! Christians do not need hex signs.

Powwow Magic

Powwow draws on many traditions of superstition and magic. It appears that some Powwow practices have similarities with Egyptian black arts and may be drawn from the secret Sixth and Seventh Books of Moses. Powwow doctors regard Moses as a famous magician rather than a prophet. This kind of magic would be used something in this manner: if a person had a cut, he would say a spell using a secret incantation drawn from the books of Moses to stop the bleeding.

I first learned of Powwow magic when Peter Wagner and I were ministering in a church in Pennsylvania. When I asked how many of the people present knew of family members who practiced Powwow magic, I was shocked at how many hands went up in the air. This kind of magic has infiltrated various evangelical denominations for years in Pennsylvania. This is sad because the sins of the fathers are visited upon the children to the third and fourth generations (see Exod. 20:5).

By the way, Peter Wagner and I learned that some witches had found out that we were coming to the Pennsylvania area and were nervous about the damage to the demonic realm done through our ministry of teaching about spiritual warfare. A leader in one of the churches overheard a few of them talking in a local store. Calling us by name, they said that they had sent e-mail messages for more curses to be cast against us and our meeting! Well, the spells did not work, because God gave us very powerful meetings during our visit. We know that the greater One lives in us!

During the times of persecution as they call it (the Salem witch-trial era), the witches went underground into the Christian church to survive. They did this by marrying Christian men, but they kept their own ways of Powwowing. While in the Church, this form of magic syncretised with Christianity through a mixture of scriptures and spells.

The Salem Witch Trials

I should include here something about the Salem trials. We have all heard about how witches were hunted down and burned at the stake until a preacher named Increase Mather and others put an end to it. These witch trials are often used as a rallying point for today's Wiccans. It is not clear exactly how many witches were killed during that time, however, is clear that some Christians who had been falsely accused of being witches were also put to death. (Furthermore, I am sure the trials made the real witches in Salem very nervous.)

WICCANS INSIST THAT IF THEY DO BAD OR BLACK MAGIC IT COMES BACK TO THEM. THEIR POEM GOES: *EVER MIND THE RULE OF THREE, WHAT YOU GIVE OUT COMES BACK TO THEE.*

Meeting in Covens

While I will not go into great detail about the witches' times of worship, I will include just a few facts. Let's start with the witch's equivalent of a cell, which is called a coven. It generally has 13 members, although this is not a hard and fast rule. Members are most concerned about the group's spiritual dynamic, what they might call energy. Former Wiccans tell me that coven members insist on the need to be in one accord. *Talk about a counterfeit of Psalm 133:1!*

One of the most sacred symbols for Wiccans is the penta-gram. It is not the same as the points-up pentacle of the Satanist—Wiccans would consider its inversion as bad as the inverted Christian cross would be to a Christian.

Bad Magic

Wiccans insist that if they do bad or black magic it comes back to them. Their poem goes: *Ever mind the rule of three, what you give out comes back to thee*. Therefore, technically, they do not do any-thing but good spells. However, some Wiccans believe in the power of cursing as is written in the book *American Folk Magick*. One curse is called, "Put it in a Jar." It instructs the Wiccan to put in a jar three rusty names, urine, fingernail clippings or a lock of hair. After this, a spell is chanted which curses a person by name and commands him to meet evil[13] and suffer whatever the Wiccan has sent as a curse.[14]

Wiccan Rituals

Different covens conduct their meetings, called *esbats*, in con-junction with the new moon, although others meet weekly or twice monthly. During these meetings the witches form a magic circle, which is like their church or holy place. In the drawing of the circle, chants are done to consecrate it as "holy ground." The circle is drawn using a magical tool, a sword called an *athame*.

Some witches work naked or "skyclad" (clad only by the sky). This is theoretically done to allow more energy to be drawn to them. The majority of covens in Europe work skyclad, but in the United States, perhaps surprisingly, a number of traditions seem to opt for wearing robes, at least during public ceremonies.[15]

Wiccans and Sex

Most Wiccan groups insist they do not conduct sexual orgies, but, sex is part of the craft for many in Wicca. There is a section in Ray Buckland's book, *Witchcraft on the Inside*, which is called "Sex Magic":

> This is one of the most potent forms of magick, for here we are dealing with much of the life forces. The sex act is obviously the best possible, and most natural, way of generating the power we need for magick.[16]

Of course, Buckland and other witches who practice this would be quick to say that no one should be forced to use this kind of magic. I do not think I have to explain to any Christian why this certainly is not holy and righteous behavior.

Even the more benign book *Teen Witch* has this to say about sexual acts:

> Witches believe that having sex with another person is not a "bad thing," although we do feel that sexual acts and interests carry a heavy responsibility.[17]

This, of course, appeals to young people who do not believe that sexual relations should only occur in the biblical confines of heterosexual marriage. This kind of Wiccan thinking is obviously very dangerous for our young people. Exodus 20:14 reads: "You shall not commit adultery."

Those who believe in worshiping gods by various names also take on the belief systems of those they worship. There is one thing that they do not understand, however, and it is that the Most High God makes the rules. We may not like them but that does not matter. He is God and that is it. We may not like the fact that our street has a traffic light the law says we are to abide by, but if we run that light, there are consequences. Sexual acts outside of a marriage relationship are sins.

Shapeshifting

Witches have familiars (demonic spirits) that are various kinds of animals. Once a witch decides which animal is to be her familiar, she bonds with it through something called shapeshifting. This is done when the person puts her hands directly over the head of the animal and slowly moves her conscious mind into the body of the animal.[18]

Shapeshifting has mainstreamed all the way down to elementary school level with the concept of *anamorph*. There are fiction books in bookstores that tell stories of kids turning into eagles and other kinds of animals. This is extremely dangerous! There are various kinds of Indian tribes that shapeshift and turn themselves into wolves and other animals.

Techno-Pagans

Today there are many kinds of pagans. One branch is filled with brilliant young scientific minds who have been dubbed "techno-pagans." They have designed games, which are in our video and toy stores, that are full of the occult. Unsuspecting parents buy these games for their children. The games mock fundamentalists and are bold in their display of witchcraft.

Folk Magic

Some writers on witchcraft specialize in Green Witchcraft, which is folk magic, fairy lore and herb craft. There are all kinds of colors of magic, from red to black.

The Goddess Movement

Certain branches of Wicca only worship the goddess. These witches are feminists and prolific writers. Go to a local bookstore and you will see rows of books about the goddess movement. They boldly proclaim that god is a she. According to Z Budapest, a popular Wiccan writer, the pure female energy generated in these circles teaches that women are whole and powerful without men. She goes on to write that nothing is out of balance and that women are healed.[19]

It is sad to say that some of these writers were raised in so-called Christian homes. Many of them suffered abuse at the hands of Christian male leaders and what they view as a patriarchal system in our churches. Let's pray that God will restore them and that they will give the one living God the true worship He deserves.

EXPOSING THE WICKEDNESS OF WICCA

According to various Wiccan writers, teenagers are the future of the craft. Satan is sly and knows that there is a tremendous revival coming. While we do not want to be persecutors of witches, we must warn our children and youth against this fast-growing source of deception. In order to do this, we must be informed. Hiding our heads in the sand will not make paganism go away.

We must not be ignorant of this device of Satan to cause hard-core idolatry to plant itself in our nations and in the hearts of the generations. Therefore, we must be prepared to give answers. As I wrote in chapter 2, divination, astrology and other occult arts are strictly forbidden in Scripture. They are an abomination to God. The people doing these things may be ignorant and truly deceived, but it does not make their practices right.

It is not my desire for Christians to persecute witches, yell at them, damage their homes or commit any violence toward them. We must never even consider such acts. None of that is Christ-like behavior. However, Wicca is a strong deception and needs to be exposed. This is a difficult thing and one that I have spent quite a bit of time praying and struggling over in my heart. I want to see Wiccans born again; but if they see an angry, mean face of Christianity, they will only turn away.

So, if you have a witch living next door, pray blessings over him or her. We are commanded to bless those who might even be cursing us. The power of blessing releases God to move in their lives.

On the other hand, Galatians 1:8 is clear when it says:

> But even if we, or an angel from heaven, preach any other gospel to you than what we have preached to you, let him be accursed.

It is not that Christians would curse Wiccans; rather, they are already separated from God because of their sin. Anyone, Wiccan or not, who does not know Christ as Savior suffers the same fate. Jesus came not to condemn us to hell but to save us from what we deserve (see John 3:17).

The next chapter will take a deeper look at the kind of divination done by psychics of today. It will include the topic of angels, which so many New Agers are talking to and releasing. Are there good angels and bad angels at work with the New Agers? We will examine the difference between their gift and the true gift of prophecy that is given by God.

Notes

1. Ed Sullivan, *School Library Journal*, October 1999, p. 48.
2. Silver RavenWolf, *TeenWitch* (St. Paul, MN: Llewellyn Publications, 1998), p. 3.
3. Ibid., p. 4.
4. Steven Lawson, interviews at the Summer Solstice celebration, Riverside, California, August 1999.
5. Ibid.
6. William Schnoebelen, *Wicca, Satan's Little White Lie* (Chino, CA: Chick Publications, 1990), p. 119.
7. Ray Buckland, *Witchcraft on the Inside* (St. Paul, MN: Llewellyn Publications, 1995), p. 32.

8. Steven Lawson, interview with Rachael Watcher, board member, Covenant of the Goddesses, San Francisco, California, August 1999.

9. Buckland, p. 32.

10. Schnoebelen, p. 38.

11. Ibid., p. 142.

12. Silver RavenWolf, p. 120.

13. Ibid., p. 110.

14. Silver RavenWolf, *American Folk Magick* (St. Paul, MN: Llewellyn Publications, 1999), p. 200-201.

15. Buckland, p. 130.

16. Ibid., p. 167.

17. Silver RavenWolf, *TeenWitch*, p. 6.

18. Ibid., p.217.

19. Buckland, quoting Z Budapest, p. 172.

CHAPTER 5

HOROSCOPES, PSYCHIC HOTLINES AND TAROT CARDS

A smiling woman pops up on our TV screen. She lures us with her psychic abilities and tries to hook us with the promise of being able to look into the future. Viewers call in by the thousands for the thrill of a psychic reading and with the hope of getting some good news. These psychic hotlines have become very popular, but they are nothing more than a contemporary form of divination.

Through the centuries, people have sought information about what will happen in their lives. There were gypsy fortune-tellers in Europe, tarot-card readers in the nineteenth century—and today we see signs in front of houses and storefronts that advertise: "Psychic reading." It is interesting to open up the book *100 Top Psychics in America* and to see how it regales readers with profiles of people who supposedly peer into the unknown and have amazing results. The book tells about Hollywood psychics,

psychics to the superstars, psychic detectives and more. Like the psychic hotlines, each of these is a form of divination.

DIVINATION

The subject of divination is so large that I could write a book on it alone. There are many different forms of divination, ranging all the way from the psychic hotlines to magic wands to "aleuromancy," which uses scattered flour, meal or tea leaves.

This chapter will include information about all kinds of divination, from that done by Nostradamus, called scrying, to tarot cards and horoscopes. Divination can be defined as the practice of peering into the future or the unknown. Christian writers John and Paula Sandford call it "Satan's copy of the gifts of knowledge and prophecy."[1]

Divination can appeal to the unbeliever and it can confuse the Christian. How do psychics know personal information about strangers? What is the difference between divination and the gift of prophecy? Should I pay to have a prophecy given to me? Let's clear up all these questions and more in this chapter.

PSYCHICS

We need to be aware of occult practices, including divination, so that we can steer clear of them and will be able to clearly articulate their dangers to those around us who dabble in them. One way that divination functions is through psychics.

The study of psychic experiences is called parapsychology. This term came into use during the late 1920s. The father of modern psychic research, J. B. Rhine, founded the Rhine Research Center that is located near Duke University in Durham, North

Carolina. This was the first of many similar organizations that have been started, many of which are connected with universities.

Scholars study many disciplines. However, it is disturbing to see that so many major universities embrace parapsychology and put tremendous resources into it. In many cases, it has gone far beyond study to actual practice, development and full-fledged endorsement of occult practices. It is one thing for university professors to analyze what Satan does; it is quite another to have them cross the line to partner in his demonic exploits. I have listed some of these centers on the accompanying chart.

Psychic Research Centers:

Anomalous Cognition Program, University of Amsterdam, The Netherlands

Cognitive Sciences Laboratory, Palo Alto, California

Consciousness Research Laboratory, Palo Alto, California

Consciousness Research Laboratory, University of Nevada, Las Vegas, Nevada

Department of Psychology, University of Hertfordshire, United Kingdom

Eotvos Lorand, University of Budapest, Hungary

Divison of Psychiatry, University of Virginia

Mind-Matter Unification Project, Cambridge
University, United Kingdom

Koestler Parapsychology Unit, University of Edinburgh,
Scotland

PEAR Laboratory, Princeton Engineering Anomalies
Research Lab, Princeton University,
Princeton, New Jersey

Institut fuer Grandzgebiete der Psychologie und
Psychohygiene, Freiburg, Germany

SRI International, Palo Alto, California[2]

Fortunes of the Rich and Famous

It is incredible to see how many well-known people have had
occult leanings. One of these was Henry Ford, the inventor of
the Model T automobile. He believed in reincarnation. Armand
Marcotte, a psychic, claims to have done readings for John Wayne
for 10 years. He also says that he did readings for Natalie Wood.
Susan Lee Shaw, another psychic, claims to channel Elvis Presley.
She was reportedly his mistress from 1963 until 1977, when he
passed away. Other psychics say they gave counsel to Marilyn
Monroe.[3]

Many stars have died tragic deaths after being involved in
the occult. I am not saying there is always a direct connection;
however, it is an eye-opening coincidence and corresponds with
Scripture.

It is not uncommon for psychics to be invited to Hollywood parties, even today. We are believing for a great revival in

Hollywood in which the stars will be hungry for the true spiritual gifts, which are only given by God.

POWER BEHIND THE PSYCHICS

According to the *Complete Idiot's Guide to Being Psychic*, 37 percent of America's urban police departments report consulting psychics in some investigations. Dorothy Allison, a well-known and controversial police psychic, led detectives to the body of a murdered girl near Niagara Falls in 1991.[4] More recently, Washington D.C. police and the FBI have had 12 to 13 leads from psychics in the Chandra Levy missing person case. "Police are taking some [psychics] quite seriously," reported Rita Cosby of Fox News.[5]

There is no doubt that sometimes psychics are charlatans and fakes out to scam people for money. But often there is real power behind the psychic manifestations of these men and women. What is the source of this "gift"? Many of the psychics will tell you that they get their channeled information from spirit guides or angels. Some even say that they consult God!

WHAT KIND OF BEINGS ARE THESE SPIRIT GUIDES? THEY ARE ACTUALLY DEMONIC BEINGS, ONLY TOO WILLING TO FEED INFORMATION TO ANYONE WHO REQUESTS IT.

What kind of beings are these spirit guides? They are actually demonic beings, only too willing to feed information to anyone who requests it. They may even cooperate with familiar, or family, spirits, which know all about the person for whom the reading is being done. The psychics, at times, will meditate until they come in contact with a spirit being which eventually becomes their spirit guide. The psychics do not understand that they are actually giving themselves over as channels of a demonic entity. I will cover more about this in chapter 9, *What! Little Ole Me Have a Demon?*

Of course, Satan, the biggest con artist of all, relishes using fakes who pose as psychics. He will do anything to get our eyes off Jesus and onto the occult.

An Angel of Light

Satan is tricky. He knows how appealing angels are to humans and he also knows that God's true angels can comfort and communicate with us. So what does Satan do? He camouflages himself as an angel of light or spirit guide!

God's angels are sent to the heirs of salvation (see Heb. 1:14). They would not give information to psychics, not even psychics with impressive credentials from major universities. The angels whom psychics receive information from are none other than angels of light, which we are warned against in 2 Corinthians 11:14-15: "And no wonder! For Satan himself transforms himself into an angel of light. Therefore it is no great thing if his ministers also transform themselves into ministers of righteousness, whose end will be according to their works." In fact, Galatians 1:8 makes it clear that we are to be on guard for any spirit that does not bear God's Word: "But even if we, or an angel from heaven, preach any other gospel to you than what we have preached to you, let him be accursed."

Many people are being demonized today when they read New Age books about angels. By demonized I mean they are giving Satan a portal into their lives. There is even a game out now called Angels. It is like a Ouiji board (see chapter 3) and supposedly helps players receive "answers" from beings masquerading as angels.

Divination in Acts

Satan's infiltration is not unique to this age. As I explained in chapter 2, the world in the day of the apostle Paul was full of the occult, including divination. The book of Acts gives us several eye-opening accounts of power encounters between believers and people empowered through the occult. One such account can be found in Acts 16:16: "Now it happened, as we went to prayer, that a certain slave girl possessed with a spirit of divination met us, who brought her masters much profit by fortune-telling."

In his commentary on the book of Acts, C. Peter Wagner states that the slave girl was demonized by a "Python spirit."[6] Wagner cites theologian Simon Kistenmaker, who argues that the best translation of this passage into English is "a spirit, namely, a Python."[7] Wagner also quotes R. C. H. Lenski, who says Python was "the mythical serpent or dragon that dwelt in the region Pytho at the foot of the Parnassumi Phocis and was said to have guarded the oracle at Delphi until it was slain by the god Apollo."[8] Wagner goes on to say that the oracle was a priestess known as the Pythia because she was empowered by the Python spirit.[9]

The spirit in the slave girl did, indeed, speak the truth saying, "These men are the servants of the Most High God, who proclaim to us the way of salvation!" (Acts 16:17). Paul, annoyed, turned and said to the spirit, "I command you in the name of Jesus Christ to come out of her" (v. 18). And it came out that very hour. This is the same Python spirit I wrote about in Chapter 2 when covering the occult presence in Ephesus.

Test the Spirits

Beloved, the story of the slave girl shows why we must test the spirits to see if they are of God. First John 4:1 clearly makes the point: "Beloved, do not believe every spirit, but test the spirits, whether they are of God; because many false prophets have gone out into the world." The devil does not mind cloaking himself as an angel of light to deceive us. He will even use what appears to be truth to suck us into his web of deceit!

It is possible for a false prophetic word given through divination to open a door to infirmities and even result in a person being cursed. I will explain this in chapter 10.

Even a person who says he or she is of God can actually be functioning through a spirit of divination. I know that this sounds rather frightening, but once you learn how to test what is true prophecy and what is given through a spirit of divination, you will realize there is nothing to fear. You must simply use discernment on what you receive from a person, even if he or she claims to be of God. How do you discern whether a prophecy is from the Spirit of God or given through a spirit of divination? Here are some guidelines drawn from my book *The Voice of God*:

1. What is the Holy Spirit giving me in the way of an inward witness? We have a precious promise from the Lord in John 10:2-5 which says that His sheep know His Voice. When the Lord speaks to us, it will give us peace and we will resonate with His Word.
2. Does the word bring glory to God? A person can tell you where you live, your doctor's name and so on, but it will be divination if the word does not bring you closer to God.[10]

A person who calls himself a Christian but who is really operating through a spirit of divination may be able to tell you many things about your life, even down to your address. But if what he or she is doing does not point to Jesus Christ, then it is false prophecy.

Sin of Balaam

In some regions in the United States, there is a serious problem when it comes to giving prophecy. Certain churches require you to give an offering of money for a prophetic word. Some churches even have a $100 line, a $50 line and a $10 line. I wonder what the difference is between the $100 prophecy and the $10 one? All of this is the sin of Balaam and should not be done.

Balaam, who seemingly started out as a prophet of God (see Num. 22:18), had a problem with the love of money. He was hired by Balak, the king of the Moabites, to curse the children of Israel. However, even through sorcery he was unable to curse what God had blessed (see Num. 24:1).

Later in life, Balaam fell into divination, became a false prophet and was killed in battle: "They [the Israelites] killed the kings of Midian with the rest of those who were killed . . . Balaam the son of Beor they also killed with the sword" (Num. 31:8).

It is confirmed in Scripture that Balaam indeed had gone away from the Lord and died: "They have forsaken the right way and gone astray, following the way of Balaam the son of Beor, who loved the wages of unrighteousness" (2 Peter 2:15).

Modern-Day Balaams

Prophets are not the only ones who fall into the sin of Balaam. I have sat in church services in which very manipulative offerings were taken. You should not be pressured to give to the extent that you feel guilty if you do not give. This is the spirit of Balaam.

Psychic Hot Lines

Have you ever wondered how the psychics on the hot lines can give such seemingly accurate information? Some are just crafty, while others have tapped into demonic spirits. Many of these psychics are adept at asking leading questions, which is an inter-rogation method called cold reading.

For example, they begin with insightful statements that could apply to a single young woman such as, "Do you have a boyfriend?" They will listen to the tone of voice and choice of words. They may even repeat what they have been told earlier in the conversation but put a small spin on it. For example, if the caller says her boyfriend is self-centered. The psychic might turn it around and later say something like this: "Your boyfriend needs to start listening to you when you are upset and when he does something that bothers you." This wording is used to make the caller think that the psychic already knew that the boyfriend never paid attention to her needs, when in reality poor commu-nication is a common problem in relationships and a self-centered boyfriend most likely would not listen.

These psychic hot lines tend to prey on and exploit those who can least afford to spend extra money. According to February 1998's *Harper's* survey, "70.2 percent of phone psychic users belong to minorities and 48.3 percent are very poor. Yet the price per minute is approximately $4."[11]

Nostradamus

One of the most famous psychics in history was Nostradamus. Born in 1503 in France, he was the eldest son in a Jewish family that later converted to Catholicism. It is said of Nostradamus that he predicted the Napoleonic Wars, the American Rev-olution, the Civil War, the assassinations of Abraham Lincoln and both Kennedys, World War II, the creation of nuclear weapons and space travel.[12] However, the way the prophecies have been interpreted stretched the facts—and always came after the fact.

Nostradamus received his visions through scrying, or gaz-ing into a bowl of water. He would place the bowl in a brass tripod, then tap his wand into the bowl, after which he touched his robe. Scrying is also what is done when people read a crystal ball or look into a mirror for answers. They gaze into the crystal ball until they either have a vision or actual images form within the ball.

This is a counterfeit of the real gift of God whereby He gives visions to His people. In fact, there are prophets called seers who receive prophetic words through visions.

The gift of prophecy is not a natural or innate gift; rather, God distributes these prophetic gifts to various people, as He chooses.

A prophet can submit his gift to God or, like Balaam, he can fall into sin and open himself up to demonic divination. The information that a prophet such as Balaam receives is not inspired by the Holy Spirit. I have seen true prophets of God who become greedy and manipulate people to give them money, thus using the gift of God for their own gain. The source of their gift then shifts to the demonic realm and eventually they can become false prophets. True prophets speak for God. Counterfeits lead people away from the one true God.

Nostradamus's information was obtained through occult methods and the source of the information was the demonic realm, even though some of it proved to be accurate.

TAROT CARDS

Another means of divination is the use of tarot cards. If you were to visit New Orleans, Louisiana, you could go to famed Jackson Square in the French Quarter and see that it is surrounded by fortune-tellers and psychics who read tarot cards. Or if you drive through any major city in the United States, on the roadside you will likely see a sign or two that read "psychic reading." The fortune-tellers inside the businesses most likely use tarot cards. This blatant use of such an abominable practice must look very strange from heaven.

Tarot History

There are differing opinions as to the origin of tarot cards. Some people believe that they originally came out of Italy in the late 1400s where renaissance schools delved into the Jewish mysticism of *Kabbalah* (received teachings) and alchemy. Others conclude that they have their roots in ancient cultures, perhaps in India, Egypt or the gypsy world that thrived along the shores of the Mediterranean.

Count de Gebelin believed tarot was rooted in the ancient world. In 1781, the Frenchman introduced the cards in his book *Monde Primitif*, which is the first recorded history of tarot.[13]

The popularity of tarot spread in the nineteenth century, particularly through the work of Eliphas Levi and, later, the secretive Hermetic Order of the Golden Dawn. Levi, who wrote the book, *The Dogma and Ritual of High Magic*, was the first person to apply to tarot the characteristics and practices of various branches of the occult, including the Kaballah and astrology.[14] The Golden Dawn expanded Levi's theories and developed a set of "magical" tarot cards that fortune-tellers still use today.

"Since its inception . . . the Hermetic Order of the Golden Dawn has continued to be the authority on the initiatory and meditative teachings of tarot," wrote Chic and Sandra Tabatha Cicero, who have developed a modern version of the Golden Dawn deck.[15]

The original Hermetic Order of the Golden Dawn, which was closely connected to masonry, enjoyed its strongest years in the late 1800s and early 1900s under the leadership of Samuel Liddell MacGregor Mathers. The order thrived until the 1970s, when the last temples were closed. However, it has seen a recent revival, with a growing number of people referring to themselves as Golden Dawn magicians.[16]

A. E. Waite and Paul Foster Case have been credited with the further advance of tarot cards and astrology mixed with numerology.

The Cards

A pack of tarot cards is made up of 78 cards, 22 of which are called the major arcana. The remaining 54 cards are minor arcana. *Arcanum*, from which the word "arcana" is derived, is the Latin word for "mysterious knowledge."[17] The major arcana are said to be the original cards.[18]

Tarot cards feature pictures of characters that suggest certain traits. For instance, the Lover's card suggests emotional success or a new love interest. There are plenty of books in any bookstore that explain each of these characteristics.

A person with a specific question or just a curiosity about the future can go to a psychic for a tarot card reading. The psychic will shuffle the deck, then give an interpretation based on how the cards are drawn. Some tarot readers lay the cards out in the Keltic form of the cross and staff.

There are many different kinds of tarot cards. One of the blackest in its occult nature is the voodoo tarot, that includes a card called Zombi. Note the way this card and its accompanying acts are described in *The New Orleans Voodoo Tarot:*

> This is an act of transgression par excellence. The victim helplessly witnesses his or her own death and then continues to live that death. The Zombi may be created by the voodooists as an act of vengeance, for service, or to serve as an example to those who would deeply transgress and strain the bonds of community.[19]

While on a visit to the city of New Orleans, I did visit the infamous Jackson Square and passed by the little tarot-reader booths that were set up surrounding the square. The presence of the occult was thick around this beautiful park in the old part of the city. Voodoo is celebrated by many people in this city as "culture." The voodoo practitioners go to the graves of former voodoo priests and priestesses and work their enchantments. It is shocking that such practices still take place in the twenty-first century. And it shows that they occur not only in developing nations but in cities everywhere.

I mentioned earlier that many people have ignorantly dabbled in the occult through reading their astrological forecasts. Unless one has been raised with the understanding that astrology is indeed witchcraft, I have found that large numbers of Christians have read their astrological forecasts in a newspaper or magazine.

Years ago I taught on the dangers of astrology at a conference in Miami. During the conference a young woman stopped me in the hall and asked, "Cindy, do you mean to tell me that God will hold me responsible for participating in witchcraft just from reading my forecast?"

"Absolutely," I answered. Scripture is clear. Isaiah 47:13-15, as I quoted earlier, talks about the judgment that comes on those who participate in such occult practices.

One thing that many believers and nonbelievers alike do not understand is that ignorance of God's law does not mean that we are not subject to it. This is, in fact, why we needed a Savior. Jesus Christ came into the world not to condemn it—because it was already condemned—but to bring it salvation (John 3:17-18).

Looking for Answers

As I have studied divination, it has become apparent that it has gotten a grip on many parts of our society. It is on our university campuses, in government, on the radio, and it is embraced by the rich and the famous. The lost are hungry to know about the future—their future! Could it be that we, the Church, have failed—and now the lost are looking for answers in all the wrong places? A sobering thought!

As the Church, we need to ask ourselves, "Why don't kings and presidents regularly consult with people who have the gifts of prophecy, discernment and wisdom? Why is it that these leaders run to mediums and psychics?" Perhaps the answer is that most world leaders have no idea that the gifts resident in the Church are available. The devil has done a better job at displaying his gifts than the Church has at making known God's gifts!

> AS THE CHURCH, WE NEED TO ASK OURSELVES, "WHY DON'T KINGS AND PRESIDENTS REGULARLY CONSULT WITH PEOPLE WHO HAVE THE GIFTS OF PROPHECY, DISCERNMENT AND WISDOM?"

Daniel's Display of Power

This was not the case in the book of Daniel. King Nebuchadnezzar had quite a display of occult power arrayed in his court—plus, he had Daniel, a prophet of the Most High God. "Then the king gave the command to call the magicians, the astrologers, the sorcerers, and the Chaldeans to tell the king his dreams. So they came and stood before the king" (Dan. 2:2).

God had given Nebuchadnezzar a disturbing dream. However, the king either forgot the dream or God was using it to show that his power was greater than the power of the astrologers, sorcerers and Chaldeans. All we know is that the king would not or could not recount the dream itself.

The occultists were dumbfounded, but Daniel had insight. How did Daniel get the answer? God answered in another dream—not through tarot cards or a crystal ball. Daniel was able to tell the King his dream and the interpretation, thus sparing his life.

Notice that Daniel never seemed afraid of the people or the occult power around him. Many times believers get scared because there is a witch who has come to church. I say, "Welcome. Come on in!" They have witchcraft but we have the Greater One living in us. Moreover, there is always the possibility that the witch has come to seek God.

I know that I can say prophetically that in the coming days there are going to be many changes in the way governments look at the Church. There will be prophets who will work with presidents and there will be kings with apostolic gifts to lead their nations. (Of course, many prophets, including me, have already met with government and business leaders at the highest levels.) Hollywood directors will have prayer meetings and seek out prophetic people rather than psychics. It will literally change the face of the world when this happens.

Christians Who Dabble

I am amazed at how many Christians have relatives who have done dowsing or water-witching and are unaware that this is an occult practice. Many Christians dabble in the occult without being fully aware of what they are doing. If you have read your horoscope, even though you may not realize it, that is dabbling in the occult. I will write more about this in chapter 10.

Scripture admonishes that "There shall *not* be found among you anyone who makes his son or his daughter pass through the fire, or one who practices witchcraft, or a soothsayer [psychic], or one who interprets omens, or a sorcerer, or one who conjures spells, or a medium, or a spiritist, or one who calls up the dead" (Deut. 18:10-11, emphasis added).

God is not mocked. Those people who do such things will eventually answer to Him for what they have done through these practices. Sadly, some of the people who practice white magic really think they are helping others by what they do.

Warnings of Judgment

The Bible strongly addresses anyone who trusts in horoscopes or goes to fortune-tellers, soothsayers or others who practice divination:

> Stand now with your enchantments and the multitude of your sorceries, in which you have labored from your youth—perhaps you will be able to profit, perhaps you will prevail. You are wearied in the multitude of your counsels; let now the astrologers, the stargazers, and the monthly prognosticators stand up and save you from these things that shall come upon you. Behold, they shall be as stubble, the fire shall burn them; they shall not deliver themselves from the power of the flame (Isa. 47:12-14).

In this age of tolerance, this Scripture may seem severe. But it is God who demands compliance, not us. Usually we will not even know when it is enforced; that is between God and the person violating His Word. But from time to time we hear about incidents resulting in the mysterious death of an occultist.

John Osteen, the long-time pastor of Lakewood Church in Houston, Texas, recounted several occasions when occultists who had taken a stand against his ministry inexplicably died.[20] I have never doubted how serious God is about this. But it really hit home a few years ago when I was ministering in South America—this passage came alive.

We were specifically praying to break the demonic powers of witchcraft over cities in Argentina when three occult leaders dropped dead (two of them were in Argentina and one was in California). They did not die because we cursed them—we did not know that they existed until after the fact and had not spoken against them as individuals. Rather they perished as God fulfilled Isaiah 47.

THE BIBLE STRONGLY ADDRESSES ANYONE WHO TRUSTS IN HOROSCOPES OR GOES TO FORTUNE-TELLERS, SOOTHSAYERS OR OTHERS WHO PRACTICE DIVINATION.

One high priestess in San la Muerte (the cult of death) in Resistencia, Argentina, actually fell asleep while smoking. She died in the fire, yet the only things destroyed in her house were her bed and the idol of San la Muerte which was five feet away from her. This news made me very sad. Unless this priestess said a last-minute prayer for salvation, she is spending her time in eternal judgment, even though she might not have believed in it!

Satan's Strategies

With the appearance of the counterculture of the 1960s and 1970s and the so-called Age of Aquarius, came a widespread interest in the occult. It was also a time when many young kids came to Jesus. As we enter the new millennium, interest in the occult is again on the rise. We are also on the verge of another great Jesus movement, and at the same time Satan is working to establish the occult with unprecedented strength to siphon off the power of this new wave of the Holy Spirit. We are simply being flooded with occult practices on every side.

Satan is certainly strategic in the ways he uses the occult to gain entrance into our everyday lives. In fact, he is downright clever. Just look where daily horoscopes are often placed in the newspaper: right next to the comic sections. As a result, children grow up reading the comics and their horoscopes. Do I think newspaper editors consult Satan about how to arrange their papers or even know they have been influenced? No, of course not. But Satan has worked so hard for so long at gaining mainstream acceptance of horoscopes that it does not take much of a nudge to get the horoscopes placed wherever he wants them.

Astrology has been accepted by many cultures for a long time. However, it does not have to maintain its place of prominence. Most newspapers have a daily horoscope column. If we pray and stand against these practices, there will be a day when they will be removed. People will no longer find them acceptable and our culture will change.

Astrology and Astronomy

Astrology and astronomy are not the same. Astronomy is the study of the planets and stars. Some astrologers use the fact that the Magi followed a star to justify the study of the heavenlies and casting a horoscope based on your birth date.

Scripture is not clear on whether these Magi were involved in the occult or whether God revealed Himself to them through a star. However, Jewish people of that time knew of the prophecy in Numbers 24:17 which promised that a star would come out of Jacob. If the Magi were from Persia, as it is surmised by some early Christian writers, they were most likely influenced by the large Hebrew settlements in their midst. Thus, the prophecies of Baalam could have been known to them.

Signs of the Zodiac

Astrologers claim to predict a person's future through the use of a birth chart. This chart is based on the time, date and place the person was born. In preparing a birth chart an astrologer will study the planets and the zodiac, which is the name of the elliptic pattern which Earth follows every year as it revolves around the sun. The zodiac is divided into 12 signs. Each person is born into one of them and is labeled by that sign. For example, a person can be an Aires or a Capricorn. Books have been written that associate specific personality traits with each of these signs.

I want to give a strong warning to anyone who dabbles in astrology. It is strictly forbidden in Scripture:

> And do not seek what you should eat or what you should drink, nor have an anxious mind. For all these things the nations of the world seek after, and your Father knows that you need these things. But seek the kingdom of God, and all these things shall be added to you (Luke 12:29-31).

This passage may appear on the surface to simply focus on having faith in God. However, in Greek "anxious mind" means "meteorize." According to *The Dake Annotated Reference Bible*, this means "to raise in mid-air," "suspend," "fluctuate," "be anxious" or "be carried about as meteors moved about with the currents, tossed up and down between hope and fear."[21] The rebuke concerns the heathen who superstitiously seek guidance by meteors, planets, signs of the zodiac, magic, witchcraft and traffic with demons in the name of astrology—all of which Scripture strictly forbids.

There are many other forms of divination. I will cover more of these occult practices—reincarnation and astral projection—in the next chapter. As you go through these chapters, be sure to use the checklist in chapter 9 that includes the things with which you have been involved, or make your own list.

Notes

1. John Sandford and Paula Sandford, *Healing the Wounded Spirit* (Tulsa, OK: Victory House, Inc., 1985), p. 293.
2. Lynn A. Robinson and LaVonne Carlson-Finnerty, *The Complete Idiot's Guide: Being Psychic* (New York: MacMillan Publishing Co., 1998), p. 49.
3. Paulette Cooper, *The 100 Top Psychics in America: Their Stories, Specialties and How to Contact Them* (New York: Pocket Books, 1996).
4. Robinson and Carlson-Finnerty, p. 12.
5. Rita Cosby, "Fox News Live with John Gibson," July 22, 2001.
6. C. Peter Wagner, *Blazing the Way* (Ventura, CA: Regal Books, 1995), pp. 70-71.
7. Ibid., p. 71.
8. Ibid.
9. Ibid.
10. Cindy Jacobs, *The Voice of God* (Ventura, CA: Regal Books, 1995), pp. 78-79.
11. Robinson and Carlson-Finnerty, p. 44.
12. Ibid., p. 25.
13. Rafal T. Prinke, "The Alchemical Tarot Deck," *The Hermetic Journal*, vol. 40, 1988, pp. 12-25.
14. Ibid.
15. Chic and Sandra Tabatha Cicero, "The Golden Dawn Magical Tarot," *Hermeticgoldendawn.org*, reprinted from *Llewellyn's New World of Mind and Spirit*, Sept.-Oct. 2000. http://www.hermeticgoldendawn.org/Gdtarot.htm (accessed June 7, 2001).
16. Chic and Sandra Tabatha Cicero, "The History of the Golden Dawn," *Hermeticgoldendawn.org*. http://www.hermeticgoldendawn.org/Gdhistory.htm (accessed June 7, 2001).
17. Merriam Webster's Collegiate Dictionary, 10th ed., s.v. "arcanum."
18. "History of Tarot Cards," *Paralumun New Age Womens Village*. http://www.paralumun.com/tarothistory.htm (accessed June 1, 2001).
19. Louis Martinie and Sallie Ann Glassman, *The New Orleans Voodoo Tarot* (Rochester, VT: Destiny Books, 1992), p. 64.
20. Steven Lawson, interview with John Osteen, Houston, Texas, 1987.
21. Finis Jennings Dake, *The Dake Annotated Reference Bible*, (Lawrenceville, GA: Dake Publishing, 1963), p. 75.

CHAPTER 6

WAS I
SOMEBODY ELSE
BEFORE
I WAS ME?

Many years ago I went to a movie that had reincarnation as its theme. I would not go to such a show today, but back then I was ignorant of most things having to do with the occult. Like many Christians, I wondered who I might have been in a former life. Fortunately, this kind of thinking did not stick around a long time with me. Yet, the fact that I ever wondered if I had been someone else shows that, in my mind, belief in reincarnation was not inconsistent with my born-again life. At the time, I did not realize that I was actually dabbling in the occult.

Likewise, I was on dangerous ground when I read my horoscope and when I played with a Ouija board. I have since repented of my participation in these practices, but my own experience demonstrates how easy it is for any one of us to stumble into the demonic realm if we are not informed.

REINCARNATION

Through the ages, people in many cultures have held the belief that they can have more than one life. Reincarnation has 4,000-year-old roots in Hinduism. Some ancient Greeks and Romans also gave credence to it. However, the Bible is clear that there is no such thing: "It is appointed for men *to die once*, but after this the judgment" (Heb. 9:27, emphasis added).

As much as some people would like it, there is no second chance. Therefore, the answer to the question "Was I someone else before I was me?" is no. We do not come back as a frog, goat or another person. We cannot return to this world to pay for the "bad karma" we created through our actions. However, we will be judged for the ways that we have sinned against God. Jesus came to pay the price for our "bad karma." Unless we repent and allow Jesus' payment (his blood on Calvary) to cover our sins, we will suffer the eternal consequences. Jesus is coming back; we cannot.

Edgar Cayce

One of the primary ways the idea of reincarnation was mainstreamed into American society was through Edgar Cayce, the so-called Sleeping Prophet. Born in 1877, Cayce, a photographer by trade, gained international recognition as a psychic. He initially claimed to receive supernatural insights about how to heal all sorts of diseases and ailments. Eventually, his work expanded to include astrological readings and revelations about past lives.

Something of an enigma, Cayce professed to be a Christian, read the Bible regularly and thought his "gift" was from God. Yet his teachings and practices clearly go against Scripture.

Cayce claimed that "the universal mind" gave him information while he was asleep or in a trance state. Wesley Harrington Ketchum, a medical doctor who knew Cayce and believed in his powers of clairvoyance, gave us this description of how Cayce received his information:

> Coming from being in direct communication with all other subconscious minds, [he] is capable of interpreting through his object mind and imparting impressions received to other objective minds, gathering in this way all knowledge possessed by endless millions of other subconscious minds.[1]

Arthur Lammers, a printer from Ohio who was interested in metaphysics and the occult, deceived Cayce, misleading him into believing that the Bible supports the teaching that we all have past lives. "Reincarnation," Lammers argued, "is simply a belief that the soul is eternal, at intervals appearing again in other physical bodies, so that it can continue as an instrument of its own development."[2]

In 1923, Cayce gave Lammers three life readings, one of which "revealed" that Lammers had been a monk in a previous life. "Beginning during the week in Dayton [visiting Lammers], the role of past lives assumed an ever-increasing prominence in Cayce's physic work and his readings, often under the questioning of those present when he went into trance, enlarged upon themes he first mentioned in the past life readings."[3]

Cayce went on to found the Association for Research and Enlightenment, located in Virginia Beach, Virginia. The organization, which promotes parapsychology and its spiritual dimensions, still uses his readings.[4]

If, as I did, you have entertained thoughts about who you would be if you were ever anyone other than yourself, this needs to be repented of, as it is an open door to demonic activity.

In studying Edgar Cayce, the premise comes home to us: Not

everything that seems spiritual is of God. The devil masquerades as an angel of light. Galatians 1:6-8 reads:

> I marvel that you are turning away so soon from Him who called you in the grace of Christ, to a different gospel, which is not another; but there are some who trouble you and want to pervert the gospel of Christ. But even if we, or an angel from heaven, preach any other gospel to you than what we have preached to you, let him be accursed.

THE BEAUTIFUL SIDE OF EVIL

Johanna Michaelsen gives sobering cautions concerning these kinds of deceptions in her book *The Beautiful Side of Evil*. Johanna tells her riveting story of how she became involved in psychic healing and other occult and New Age practices. The narrative of her early life is worth reading because it is, among other things, a classic example of how generational spirits or familial spirits are passed along in family lines. I gleaned much of the following information from her book.[5]

Johanna's Story

Johanna had an Aunt Dixie who was a trance medium and very much involved in spiritualism. (I will write more about spiritualism later in this chapter.) During Aunt Dixie's seances, faces of the dead would materialize on the wall and the entire house would shake and rattle as though in the grip of a giant terrier. She would awaken from her trance with a blinding headache, having no memory of the events that had transpired. One family member recollected that Aunt Dixie, while in a trance, could find lost articles and had tremendous strength. She died sometime in the 1920s, alone, forgotten and a pauper.[6] I have noted that many people deeply involved in spiritualism tend to be desolate when they die.

Johanna found out in 1975 that her aunt had predicted that someone in her generation would inherit her powers. The pattern for Johanna's life is very similar to others whose descendents have been involved in spiritualism. You might recognize the pattern in your own life. At an early age, Johanna heard spirits manifesting themselves in her house. There were doors slamming, heavy footsteps and other noises. Some spirits appeared to her with horrid manifestations of such things as a bloody, severed head.

> JUST AS GOD HAS A PLAN FOR EACH OF US, SO DOES SATAN. THIS IS ESPECIALLY TRUE FOR THOSE WITH THE CALL OF GOD TO BE A PROPHET.

Johanna was very close to a church leader who had lost his son and, in his grief, turned to spiritualism. She began to dabble in the occult herself. Sadly, she made her leap into the demonic realm while attending a Wesleyan college, where she was labeled a witch because she wore black most of the time. This is a good lesson for all Christians. We need to be careful that we do not call a person a witch just because of what he or she wears. Such a label could very well tip that person over the edge, as in Johanna's case.

It is eye-opening to note how once Satan targets a particular person, he begins to work at demonizing the person through circumstances and relationships. Just as God has a plan for each of us, so does Satan. This is especially true for those with the call of God to be a prophet. Satan will try to pull them into telepathy or convince them that they are mediums. People can get sucked into occult practices if they do not have proper training. In our churches, we need to inform people about the dangers of introductory occult practices such as astrology. The Church must lay a biblical foundation for its members and teach against the occult.

The Lure of Mind Control

Eventually, Johanna got into mind control. The Silva Method teaches people to function at will using the alpha brain wave. The training is divided into courses, each one moving the student to a higher level. The first course (level one) is titled "Controlled Relaxation." This sounds good to unbelievers because they are told that they will be able to sleep and awaken at will and that they will no longer suffer from maladies such as severe headaches. José Silva popularized his method, founding Silva International in Laredo, Texas, in 1966. But this sounds similar to the trances Cayce went into when he communicated with the spiritual world.

The next course, at the second level, is "General Self-Improvement." People are taught how to stop smoking or overeating. They are also told that they will be able to control any kind of pain or bleeding. It is not hard to see why desperate people would run to such a course. However, the Church, through the gifts of the Holy Spirit, should be the one with the answers to these needs, not an occult group. Sadly, a powerless Church drives people to run after an alternate power.

The study of mind control opened the door to the generational spirit from Johanna's Aunt Dixie to work in a full-blown way in her life. As she began to investigate alternate powers, she invited two spirit guides into her life—Jesus and Mamacita. Spirit guides are actually demonic beings that pose as helpful spirits or angels and promise to protect and direct those who surrender themselves. It is particularly alarming to realize that the angels of light will masquerade as Jesus Himself! There are many spirits who would take the name of Jesus, but they are not Jesus of Nazareth. These false Jesuses cannot bring salvation to anyone.

Psychic Surgery

Johanna's mind-control teacher told her of a woman in Mexico City named Pachita, who attained level seven and performed amazing healings. Pachita had a spirit guide named Hermanito Cuauhtemoc (which means "little brother of Cuauhtemoc") who actually did the healing.

Johanna visited Pachita and Hermanito, who inhabited Pachita's body. She was astounded as she watched Hermanito do psychic surgeries with a rusty knife. He would cut into a body and throw out the tumor—with amazing results. Hermanito would even say that it was only with god's help that he did these operations. *However, we must ask ourselves, which god?*

Johanna became increasingly disillusioned because the healing cures performed through the occult were only temporary. While it may seem that a person is healed through an occult act, Satan never brings life; he only brings death. I have observed that those who go to occult healers actually become inhabited with a demonic "healing spirit" that cooperates with the spirit of infirmity and causes the symptoms to subside for a season. They fake a total healing, only to turn against the sick person at a later time and kill them. James 1:15 declares that sin, when it is full-grown, brings death.

Actor Andy Kaufman sought a psychic healing after being diagnosed with lung cancer. However, Ramon Labo, who charged huge amounts for his services in the Philippines, turned out to be a fraud, and Kaufman died shortly after returning to the United States. In cases like this one, Satan does not need a healing spirit to work his deception. He simply gets the person to place his or her faith in the psychic healer rather than in Jesus.

Discovering Jesus of Nazareth

Johanna became very eclectic in her belief system, mixing Hinduism, spiritualism and Christianity. She also began practicing yoga. All along, Johanna thought she was following Jesus Christ because of the name of her spirit guide! Her freedom in Christ eventually came after she visited the L'Abri Fellowship in Switzerland and was taught by Os Guinness that there was only one God and His Name was Jesus Christ of Nazareth—the One who is God uniquely incarnate in the flesh.

> But I fear, lest somehow, as the serpent deceived Eve by his craftiness, so your minds may be corrupted from the simplicity that is in Christ. For if he who comes preaches another Jesus whom we have not preached, or if you receive a different spirit which you have not received, or a different gospel which you have not accepted, you may well put up with it! (2 Cor. 11:3-4).

The spirits holding Johanna captive did not want to let go. They tried to torment, intimidate and destroy her. However, the power of the Greater One, the true Jesus, through the shedding of His precious blood, made provision for her to be set free.

See chapter 9 for the steps to renouncing spirit guides.

SPIRITUALISM

When asked how a person could become a millionaire, railroad baron Commodore Vanderbilt once told a reporter, "Do as I do. Consult the Spirits!"[7] Concerning the stock of the Central

Pacific Railroad, he added, "It's bound to go up . . . Mrs. Woodhull said in a trance."[8]

Spiritualism, also called spiritism, is deeply imbedded in the history of the United States. Vanderbilt was a dedicated spiritualist, one of an estimated 10 million in the United States in the post-Civil-War decade.[9] This era saw great fanaticism with its roots intertwined into the women's rights movement. Not all members of the woman's rights movement were spiritualists, but the cause was inseparable from spiritualism.[10]

Raps in the Night

Spiritualism is a religion that sometimes mixes Christian teachings with the occult. In spiritualism, a medium goes into a trance to consult the dead. Cayce was a spiritualist medium.

Spiritualism was popularized in the United States by the Fox sisters of Arcadia, New York. Their supernatural encounters reportedly all started in 1848 when they heard raps, bumps and other nocturnal noises. When Kate Fox was 11 years old she talked with unseen spirits. As she communicated with the spirits, she developed a system of raps. At first, a particular rap was a "yes" answer from the spirits. This grew to the point where the number of raps corresponded with certain letters of the alphabet. Eventually, the people involved would fall into trances and the spirits would speak through them.

Other raps were reported in nearby Rochester. When word got out, curious people would pack the buildings where the raps had been heard. The spirits identified themselves as people who had died and "passed over" into the other world. The Bible warns us about these seducing spirits and doctrines of demons (see 1 Tim. 4:1-4).

Early Spiritualist Influences

Sadly, once the Pandora's box of spiritualism had been opened, it quickly spread to England and went around the world.

Intrigued by the reports out of upstate New York, many people turned to the teachings of Emanuel Swedenborg, a Swedish philosopher and spiritualist forerunner to the Fox sisters. Swedenborg had fallen into a trance in 1750 and claimed to have seen the spirit world. He told people that in the other realm men were able to have both wives and concubines. *No wonder his teachings appealed to so many!*

On the other end of the spectrum, Elizabeth Cady Stanton, a pioneer of the women's suffrage movement, also consulted the spirits and claimed to have heard raps in her home. Cady was instrumental in the first women's rights convention in Seneca Falls. How much has this occult tie affected the feminist movement both in its beginning stage and today? That is anyone's guess. However, it is important to note that not all the women's suffrage leaders were involved in the occult. Frances E. Willard, as I wrote in my book *Women of Destiny*, was called of God to fight for a woman's right to vote because women could use that right to protect the home.

By 1858, spiritualism had spread abroad and Allen Kardec had become one of the most visible leaders of the movement in Europe. He wrote books, led conferences and started the Parisian Society of Psychical Research.

Counterfeit Spirits

One of the most enlightening books I have read on spiritualism is *Challenging Counterfeits* by Raphael Gasson. He shows how the Fox sisters eventually turned to drinking and completely lost all sense of moral responsibility. He shares how Margaret Fox, in the presence of her sister, Kate, at an anti-spiritualist meeting in 1888, declared, "I am here tonight, as one of the founders of spiritualism, to denounce it as absolute falsehood—the most wicked blasphemy the world has ever known."[11] Margaret later recanted the admission, but doubt about spiritualism had set in.[12]

DELIVERANCE FROM SPIRITUALISM

Earlier I noted how those with a call of God upon their lives are especially sought out by Satan. He wants to suck them into the occult. One of those whom Satan tried to ensnare is now the leader of one of the largest deliverance ministries in the world, Cleansing Stream. This ministry is led by an anointed leader named Chris Hayward and is associated with the respected Foursquare pastor Jack Hayford.

God uses Chris in a special way to set captives free, and he is able to teach others how to do what he does. One day, while in a meeting of the Apostolic Council of Deliverance Ministries headed by C. Peter Wagner, I told Chris I was writing this book and asked his advice.

Meet Chris Hayward

Chris proceeded to tell me that he had been caught up in spiritualism as a young man and had adamantly believed that what he was doing was right. His story is fascinating because, like Johanna Michaelsen, the enemy pulled him in through deception.

Chris was raised in a Christian family, but once they left their homeland of England his parents drifted away from the Lord. For a while, the Haywards attended a lifeless church. Then, when Chris was 14, though not yet born again, he became hungry for truth. He picked up some Edgar Cayce books and read about reincarnation. At the age of 16, he found out about a place in California called Joshua's Temple. Curious, he went to visit. The temple was headed by a man who would go into a trance state, and "Joshua" would speak through him.

At that time, Chris started doing odd jobs for a lady who had an occult library. One day he asked her, "Do you believe in reincarnation?" I can just imagine that Satan had worked hard to position Chris in just that place to set him up for a deep deception. The lady was only too glad to help him and supply him with books on reincarnation and other occult subjects.

Chris continued going to the Joshua Temple. He learned how to go into a trance state and became an apprentice medium. One day, he questioned something the leader had said, and the spirit that controlled him spoke: "You need to listen to me! You need to listen to what I say!" One thing that happens in these cults is that the leaders, who are full of pride, want to maintain absolute control over the lives of their followers.

A Spiritual Breakthrough

This encounter really shook Chris, and he began to doubt the truth of what was happening around him. However, he was still deeply deceived. "I would have died for what I believed [about spiritualism]," Chris told me.[13]

Chris went into the army, where he became a chaplain's assistant. While in Vietnam, he was born again through a missionary who had served in the field for 30 years. While Chris prayed to receive Christ, he still had to go through the process of walking out of the occult side of his belief system. The spirits controlling him did not want to give him up, and the battle was great. Chris recounted how on two occasions the spirits attempted to physically overpower and suffocate him. He now laughs off those incidents as parlor tricks of the enemy meant to deter him from following Christ.[14]

Later, Chris went to visit the woman who had loaned him her occult library and to tell her about the Lord Jesus. He had never faced such an intense sense of evil in his life, no doubt from the spirits around the woman—and that was a woman in her 80s!

Chris eventually went to work with Walter Martin, who wrote *Kingdom of the Cults,* and God later led him to the ministry he heads today, working with more than 2,500 churches in the United States and in more than 50 nations. Each year, more than 50,000 people are personally ministered to in the area of deliverance through Cleansing Stream. And, to his delight, Chris's parents have also become strong disciples of Jesus Christ.

TALKING TO THE DEAD

The deception of spiritualism not only ensnared Chris, but it traps many others. People often start the process of becoming a medium because they have a sincere desire to help people who are in grief. They believe they can assist people by talking with a dear departed loved one. What they do not realize is that mediums do not talk to the dead; rather, they commune with demons.

In his book *Challenging Counterfeits*, author Raphael Gasson gives some insights into how a medium goes into a trance state. The medium will breathe heavily, then suddenly stop breathing altogether until the spirit guide enters the body to speak. This only takes a few split seconds from the time the medium stops breathing. The medium's body becomes cold to the touch, as if dead, and when the spirit speaks through the medium, it uses the vocal organs of the body that it is possessing. The voice of the medium changes into the recognizable accents of the spirit guide—recognizable, that is, after a little acquaintance with the guide. The medium himself is not conscious of anything that is being said or done. He or she is merely a channel for the spirit guide. The people in attendance sense the spirit's presence either by cool breezes, which seem to spread around the room, or by heat permeating likewise.[15]

Psychometry

One type of spiritualist phenomena is called psychometry. This practice is regarded as the power to make personal contact with a living person who is in a geographically different location from the person seeking the connection. It can be an attempt to make contact with the spirits of the dead. Practitioners teach that psychometry is accomplished by handling something, such as an article of clothing, that belongs the person they seek to contact. These psychic detections are often used in attempts to locate a missing person.

Ectoplasmic Mass

There are different types of medium activities or mediumships. When a spirit simply speaks through a person, it is called a *mental* mediumship. When others in the room can see or perceive the activity, which is an ectoplasmic mass, it is called a *physical* mediumship.

Anyone who has watched horror movies has probably seen Hollywood's version of ectoplasmic mass. Spiritualists claim that it is a semi-luminous, thick vapor which oozes from the medium's mouth, ears, nose, eyes or stomach and is dimly visible in the gloom. This mist gradually becomes solid as it makes contact with the natural surroundings of the seance room.[16]

Gasson reports that when touched, the ectoplasmic mass will move back into the body or, if suddenly seized, the medium will scream or become violently ill. A medium who suddenly grabs this mass can suffer physical injury or even die. Gasson, a former occultist, wrote, "I myself was blinded for nearly 24 hours after such an incident."[17]

These ectoplasmic masses will take the shape of the face of a person and actually look at someone seated in the room. This apparition appears as a strange phenomena, sometimes taking on the color of the dead person's eyes.

The strongest form of this kind of seance is "materialization." This takes place when the ectoplasmic mass forms a full body and the spirit actually walks around until it finds the person with whom it wants to speak. The formed mass is supposedly the spirit of a person who is dead. Animals will also appear and take on the form of a human.

Test the Spirits
Such a manifestation is not a dead person come back, but it is a spirit. We must always test the spirits:

> Beloved, do not believe every spirit, but test the spirits, whether they are of God; because many false prophets have gone out into the world (1 John 4:1).

It is extremely sad that loved ones could become so desperate and deceived as to seek to contact those who have died. Grieving without having the power of God to console you is a desolate place indeed.

Western culture is infected with the thinking that everyone who dies goes to some nice kind of afterlife regardless of what they did on Earth. This is commonly held and a great deception.

SPIRITUALISM TODAY

You may think that spiritualism is a limited practice in today's modern culture. Not so! Even if there is not spiritualism on highly developed levels as it was in the late 1800s, there is quite a bit of syncretistic belief among the people in the United States and other countries as well. Some people who live in the hills of West Virginia, in parts of Texas and other places around the country still use aspects of spiritualism on a regular basis.

Author Chuck Pierce has related to me how he once saw his grandfather speak a chant into his hand.[18] He then pointed to a bunch of wasps and they all dropped dead! He also told me that it was normal in his family if something had gone wrong to see if you had violated any superstitious belief. Chuck tells of severe migraine headaches he would get when he was 24. When he lay down to rest he remembered a chant his grandmother would have him say against headaches. After becoming a Christian, he realized that this had been an occult practice, but he had never specifically repented of the chants.

A spirit can live in the flesh without total possession of the person. We are a three-part being: spirit, soul and body. A spirit would have to take over all three parts to completely possess a person. This cannot happen to a believer, because our spirit dwells with the Holy Spirit. However, it is possible and common for a Christian to be oppressed by a spirit that controls or influences the soul or mind, the will or the emotions. The Holy Spirit will not violate our free will. If we give place to the occult in our minds, we open ourselves to the possibility that demonic powers will oppress us.

Chuck was not possessed by Satan. He was oppressed. His participation in the occult (through the chants) gave Satan the right to oppress him, and this oppression was manifested through the

> THE HOLY SPIRIT WILL NOT VIOLATE OUR FREE WILL. IF WE GIVE PLACE TO THE OCCULT IN OUR MINDS, WE OPEN OURSELVES TO THE POSSIBILITY THAT DEMONIC POWERS WILL OPPRESS US.

headaches. Moreover, the spirit that oppressed him appeared to be a familial, or a familiar spirit. Some spirits leave when occult involvement is denounced, but some have to be told to leave.

Chuck denounced the chants and immediately felt a familiar spirit leave his body. He was cured of headaches from that day!

Astral Projection

Another occult practice that can be found today is that of astral projection, or out-of-body experience. Astral projection uses something similar to ectoplasmic mass for out-of-body travel, but it is called "astral substance."

In astral projection, what is called the "gross astral" remains with the body to keep it functioning while part of its substance projects (or leaves) to form the astral body. Practitioners believe that the connection to the gross astral must remain or the person will die. This connection is made by maintaining a lifeline called "the silver cord." Oddly enough, this name was taken from Ecclesiastes 12:6 which refers to a silver cord being loosed. The silver cord in Ecclesiastes refers to death!

Astral exercises begin by focusing on the *chakras,* or energy centers of the body (the crown, brow, throat, heart, solar plexus, navel and genitals) and Earth. Visualization is used to see light coming from these areas. Eventually the person will imagine psychic energy flowing from his or her body to form an astral body.

The Watcher

At first, the student is taught to form a watcher. A watcher is sent to the person whom the student wants to visit or to the person from whom the student wants to obtain knowledge. This is done entirely without the permission of the person being "watched." I have found that this is one way members of the occult find out the whereabouts of Christians or gain knowledge of what they are doing. This has happened to me and my associates on more than one occasion, although it happens less frequently now, because we have sent the watchers scurrying back with a strong rebuke.

A person who practices astral projection will likely believe that the watcher is an extension of his astral self. However, it is most likely a familiar spirit that goes forth to gather information and bring it back.

In Weatherford, Texas, where my husband and I once lived, I was helping a young man involved in a coven break free from his occult past. As we began to address the problem directly, we began to experience spiritual warfare. Specifically, we had occult visitations. Sometimes the spirits would actually come in the form of a large, all-seeing eye (or third eye). In the spirit realm, the intercessors who had gathered at my house and I could see it floating. We would command the eye to be blinded and send it back to where it came from. At other times the watcher spirits would spy through the use of familiars, which I discussed in chapter 4.

Spiritualists claim that the watcher forms a vehicle in which the conscious mind can travel; some call it soul travel. At times this watcher comes in the form of an animal, particularly when astral travel is practiced by a Satanist. But some occultists consider such symbolism to be dangerous.

Out-of-Body Travels

People at the most advanced stage of astral projection claim the ability to actually form an astral body; the watcher is usually a more elemental, spherical body. In this practice, a person lies down and visualizes a silver-gray mist coming out of one of the chakras and forming what is called a key figure. After this is formed, the person continues the exercise by sending his or her consciousness into the key figure.

This key figure is kept attached to the body by the silver cord. Astral-projection practitioners contend that if too much astral mass is used, the people they might want to visit will more readily know they are there, and the mass might snap back into the body and traumatize it.

A Personal Encounter

Years ago we were in the Seattle area praying and became aware of a large, New-Age community. One particular man was in the forefront of a parade as they marched down the street chanting "take back the ground the Christians have taken."

I was staying in the home of the women in charge of the organization that had invited me into the city. One day I happened to walk past her bedroom. I was startled to see a wiry man with salt-and-pepper hair. He wore glasses and was dressed in blue polyester pants with a black belt and a shirt.

I went into the kitchen and commented to my hostess that I was not aware that her husband had come home and that I would like to meet him. She looked quite surprised and commented that he would not be home for some time. I immediately went back to the bedroom and rebuked the "person" who had astral-projected himself into the home. Later, I found out that the man I had seen fit the exact description of the head of the New-Age movement in the area and was the man who had led the chants against Christians.

It is hard to tell whether some of the experiences called "out-of-body," such as the one I have mentioned here, are real or are simply lying wonders. Satan is able to cause extremely realistic counterfeit experiences, so at times it may be difficult to determine what is actually going on in the spiritual realm. One example of this is what happens to us in our dreams; some of them seem so real yet they are actually happening in a dream state.

I want you to know that we do not have to be afraid of these kinds of encounters, but rather they should provide the opportunity for us to come into a deeper realization of the protection afforded to us by our life in Christ Jesus. The more we know our authority in the heavenly realms, the less we will be harassed either by astral projectors or by demonic entities.

Astral Sex

Some occultists claim that "astral sex" is extremely gratifying, since a woman or man could visit someone else without his or her knowledge and establish sexual contact.[19] This type of contact is often given over to the what is called the incubus (male) or succubus (female) spirit.

Given what we know about astral travel, we cannot discount dreams that become extremely sexual—we might have been visited by someone in astral form.

This, of course, is the height of invasion of privacy and should never be done! If you are bothered by something similar to this, pray over your room before sleeping and ask the Lord to protect you with His angels. I have also found the reading of Psalm 91 out loud to be most helpful and protective.

At one time or another, you might have been aware of a presence in your room. Sometimes you might hear or sense a sighing or even feel like you have been physically pushed. There have been times that I have been hit hard by an astral body and momentarily stunned. It is possible that this is not really an astral body but a demon that has been given the right to attack you by those performing the so-called astral projection.

I have found that attacks from the spirit realm have lessened in my life the more that I have learned the authority that I have through the name of Jesus Christ. The epilogue has a special section on the authority of the believer that will help you as you grow in this area of your Christian life.

While You Sleep

While it may seem strange that demonic spirits can attack in this way, even while a person is sleeping, if you would stop a moment and think about it, why would Satan not come at us from all fronts?

Have you ever had a terrible nightmare that has awakened you in the middle of the night? There are times when this sort of dream comes because you have been under demonic attack.

How do you know if that is the case? For one, if the dream is sexual in nature you will think thoughts such as, *I would never do that!* or *I wonder where that came from.* You will usually feel quite defiled by the experience.

As the subject of this chapter indicates, demons are real beings that can and do try to attack Christians. If you feel that you have had such an attack it is important that you pray for yourself, or even better, ask someone else to pray with you to break any demonic attachments that may have occurred during the dream.

> IT IS CRITICAL TO HAVE PRAYER BOTH TO BREAK THE POWER OF OPPRESSING SPIRITS AND TO CLEANSE YOURSELF OF THE DEFILEMENT THEY BRING.

It is critical to have prayer both to break the power of these oppressing spirits and to cleanse yourself of the defilement they bring. If this is not done, the enemy will try to use these dreams against you to lead you into some kind of sexual temptation.

Let me give you an example how this works: Satan will send demons of lust, perversion or fantasy to try to open a door for him to send along a temptation to get you to fall into sin. The incubus spirit (which takes the form of a male) and the succubus spirit (which takes the form of a female) will try to sexually arouse you in your dreams. At times, people say that they even feel that such a spirit has actually laid on top of them.

This spirit will attach itself to you. From there its job is to send perverted thoughts into your mind. If you at all let your mind dwell on these thoughts, or if you have any generation iniquities of lust, then these start to work together to form a stronghold.

The next step Satan takes is to send an actual person to tempt you to fall into sin. If you have been bombarded by these spirits and are in a vulnerable place, some in their weakened conditions actually succumb to the temptation.

Here is a sample prayer to break the demonic attachments:

In the name of Jesus Christ of Nazareth, I break all the power
of all sexual spirits that were sent against me in the night.
I command you in the name of Jesus to be gone from me.
Father, I now ask that You cleanse me from all the defilement
that has come from this demonic attack.
In the name of Jesus. Amen.

Make sure that you stay in the Word after this time and are pure in your thought life. If the attack comes again against your mind or body, resist the devil and he will flee from you.

The next chapter is on Satanism. We as the Body of Christ do not know very much about this area, although deliverance counselors are rescuing people from the clutches of the demonic beings which hold satanic ritual abuse victims in bondage. Again, I want to reiterate that we do not need to fear these things. God has not given us a spirit of fear, but of power and of love and of a sound mind (see 2 Tim. 1:7).

In this chapter we have looked at some heavy, eye-opening information. But I do not want any Christian going away in fear. I suggest you now pray something along the lines of this cleansing prayer:

Father God, I now ask you to cleanse my mind and heart from any defilement from reading this chapter. I also bind Satan in the Name of Jesus from any spiritual attachments from the demonic realm through any open door that I might have in my thought life or the sins of my fathers. In Jesus' Name. Amen.

Notes

1. Jess Stearn, *Edgar Cayce the Sleeping Prophet* (New York: Bantam Books, 1967), p. 6.
2. Ibid., p. 10.
3. J. Gordon Melton, "Edgar Cayce and Reincarnation: Past Life Readings as Religious Symbology," *California Institute of Integral Studies*, article originally appeared in *Syzygy: Journal of Alternative Religion and Culture* (vol. 3, no. 1-2, 1994). http://www.ciis.edu/cayce/melton.html (accessed June 19, 2001).
4. Stearn, p. 343.
5. Johanna Michaelsen *The Beautiful Side of Evil* (Eugene, OR: Harvest House, 1982).
6. Ibid., p. 16.
7. Barbara Goldsmith, *Other Powers* (New York: Random House, 1998), p. XI.
8. Ibid.
9. Ibid.
10. Ibid.
11. Raphael Gasson, *Challenging Counterfeits* (South Plainfield, NJ: Bridge-Logos, 1985), p. 48.
12. "Fox Sisters," *Electric Library*. http://www.encyclopedia.com/printable/17385.html (accessed July 3, 2001).
13. Chris Hayward, personal interview with author, n.d.
14. Ibid.
15. Gasson, p. 86.
16. Ibid., p. 130.
17. Ibid.
18. Chuck Pierce, personal interview with author, n.d.

19. Melita Denning and Osborne Phillips, *Astral Projection* (St. Paul, MN: Llewellyn Worldwide, 1999), p. 203.
20. Cindy Jacobs, *Possessing the Gates* (Tarrytown, NY: Chosen Books, 1991), pp. 140-143.

CHAPTER 7

BLACK MAGIC

Caution: The material in this chapter is not meant to be read by young children. It has content which might produce fear in them. However, mature adult believers should not be afraid, because Scripture admonishes us to not be ignorant of Satan's devices. The God whom we serve is able to protect and cleanse us of any defilement that might come as we read about black magic and other occult practices.

On April 11, 1989, a bizarre and horrific discovery was made on a remote ranch west of the Mexican city of Matamoros, just across the border from Brownsville, Texas. Twelve bodies were exhumed. When authorities did a thorough search of what became known as Devil Ranch, three more bodies were found and an eclectic collection of satanic ritual objects was discovered.

One of the victims was a young University of Texas premed student named Mark Kilroy. Mark had met a young coed while he was barhopping during spring break. Only later was it learned that he had been kidnapped to be used as human sacrifice in a dark Afro-Caribbean religious ritual.[1]

It later came to light that the cult had targeted Mark because he was an Anglo-American. The group's leader, Adolfo de Jesus

Constanzo, felt that the death of a young white male would secure supernatural protection for his drug deals on American soil.[2]

Mark's death was brutal. He was killed with a blow from a machete to the head and his legs were cut off. His brain was used in the ceremony, and his body parts were mixed with blood from animals, then boiled in an iron kettle. Cult members drank the blood, believing it would make them unconquerable. This ritual was black magic.

SATANIC CRIMES

This gruesome discovery came as quite a shock to critics who had downplayed satanic crimes and accused fanatic Christian fundamentalists of exaggerating the threat. However, Mexico is not the only place where satanic rituals have become deadly. Police departments across the United States continue to receive reports of devil worship, secret rituals and occult-related violence.

It has happened in big cities and in small quiet towns such as Joplin, Missouri. Joplin may be the last place anyone would ever think a satanic murder would take place, but it did.

A Joplin teenager, Pete Roland, became involved in Satanism along with his friends, Jim Hardy and "Eddie." As they moved deeper into the demonic realm, they filled their minds with the sounds of heavy metal music from groups such as Mötley Crüe, Black Sabbath, Metallica, Megadeath and Slayer. They were soon inspired to kill small animals. But that was only the beginning. In the book *Painted Black,* Eddie tells of the trio's complete devotion to Satan:

Satan for satanists is as God is to Christians. (For them) Satan knows all, sees all. As with God, Satan demands souls. Satanists are taught: "We are here to collect enough souls so Satan can draw on them to win the battle with God and get back the throne which is rightfully his. One of these days Satan will have a sufficiently large army, and the biblical Armageddon will commence. On the other hand, 'There is no absolute timetable' for the Satanic apocalypse."[3]

These boys chose a soul to collect for Satan. Their target was Steven Newberry. He was selected because he was deemed not worthy to live. Sadly, Steven's mother told how he had been obsessed with the notion that his cronies were going to get rid of him. He even composed a story about being at the bottom of a well, looking up at the face of Jim Hardy. Other students at school knew he was on a hit list, and the police even knew that there was some satanic activity taking place in the area.

SATANISM COMES IN MANY FORMS. SOME IN THE BLACK OR OCCULT ARTS OPENLY ADMIT THEY SERVE THE DEVIL; OTHERS DENY HIS LITERAL EXISTENCE YET USE HIS NAME.

None of that prevented Hardy, Roland and Eddie from acting upon their satanic beliefs. Steven Newberry was captured, bludgeoned to death with baseball bats and thrown down a well. Why did they do it?

One possible reason is that their minds had become "metal-lined" from listening to lyrics that promote graphic violence, death and torture. Abundant drug use was another likely culprit. Obviously, these three youths had become out of touch with reality.

While I never met any of the assailants in person, from what I have read and heard it is fair to conclude that they were demonized. They were desensitized through music, drugs and satanic rituals. In one of the rituals, Hardy taught Roland to defecate upon a Bible, a traditional satanic gesture harking back to the black masses of the fifteenth century. Hardy confided in Roland that the power he had would increase tremendously if he could kill a person.[4] This is very similar to the psychology that had operated within the Matamoros cult.

A Wake-Up Call
Why have I included all of these gruesome details? Sometimes we need a reality check. I do not have a desire to sensationalize the dark side of the occult, yet I do not want another parent to ever lose a child to the occult. There is an educational process that anyone who has a child or loves children needs to go through. We ought to familiarize ourselves with the history, signs and belief systems of black magic and Satanism.

BRANCHES OF SATANISM

Satanism comes in many forms. Some in the black or occult arts openly admit they serve the devil; others deny his literal existence yet use his name. A third group describes spirit guides or supernatural beings but stops short of identifying these spirits as satanic. A plethora of satanic groups exist, with some such as the Church of Satan offering a formal membership. Many Satanists such as Roland, however, operate in a self-styled mode that draws from many sources to create their own diabolic belief system.

Satanic practices in these groups range from unabashed hedonism to malicious spell casting to human sacrifice.

Anger Toward Christians

It is peculiar to note that most of these groups involved in black magic and overt Satanism never level attacks against Hindus, Buddhists or people of other religions—they only target Christianity. There seems to be a great anger aimed toward God and anyone connected with Him. People in these groups seem to have a desire to tear down everything for which Christianity stands.

THE CHURCH OF SATAN

Disdain of Christianity was certainly found in Anton LaVey, the founder of the Church of Satan. We only have to read the story of his life to know that he was angry at the Church and at God. LaVey, who claims that at one time he played the organ for a carnival and for tent revival meetings, had this to say about believers:

> On Saturday night, I would see men lusting after half-naked girls dancing at the carnival, and on Sunday morning when I was playing organ for tent-show evangelists at the other end of the carnival lot, I would see these same men sitting in the pews with their wives and children, asking God to forgive them and purge them of carnal desires. And the next Saturday night they'd be back at the carnival or some other places of indulgence. *I knew then that the Christian church thrives on hypocrisy*, and that man's carnal nature will win out no matter how much it is purged or scourged by any white-light religion (emphasis added).[5]

Who would have imagined how the sin of so-called believers would turn one 18-year-old boy away from what might have been a life of serving Jesus Christ and thrust him into the role of starting the Church of Satan! This is sobering. We do not know who is in church with us or who we might meet each day. Therefore, it is our responsibility to always live a holy life. We must do this not only to please God and move forward in our own spiritual walk but also to be a constant testimony of faithfulness to others.

Auspicious Beginning

LaVey founded his Church of Satan on April 30, 1966, in San Francisco, California and became known as the Black Pope. He chose that specific date because it is a major occult holiday called Walpurgisnacht. Even though it is not directly related, it is interesting to note that Adolph Hitler committed suicide on April 30, 1945. This coincidence becomes eerie when we consider that it has been fully documented that Hitler's practice of the black arts was vital to the existence of the Third Reich.[6]

The Church of Satan was officially recognized as a religion by the United States military in 1967 and, later, given even more recognition when a Navy seaman requested a satanic funeral upon his death. This funeral was done with a full Navy honor guard, with none other than LaVey himself officiating.

We get further insight into LaVey's life when we look at his family history. While there is no concrete evidence, he claimed that he was the descendant of a gypsy grandmother from Transylvania, which, of course, is where the infamous real-life Count Dracula lived. If this story is true, she no doubt passed along legends of vampires and witches and possibly some familiar spirits. From her, LaVey most likely developed his love for books about Dracula and vampires.

The Satanic Bible

The Satanic Bible defines the tenets of the basics of the Satanic belief system. According to this book, true Satanists do not believe in a literal devil or Satan. Instead, to them, the devil is the dark force in nature that human beings are just beginning to fathom.

However, in my study of Satanists, I have found that they contradict themselves. While many say Satan is simply a dark force in nature, they also refer to Satan as a deity. They address him as a real entity in salutes such as, "Hail, Satan!"

The core of the Church of Satan belief system is hedonism in its most extreme form. Members admit that their version of Satanism is a blatantly selfish and brutal philosophy. It is their belief that some of the violence in our society comes from people who do not let their own animal natures take their course. They do not, as a general rule, believe in the hereafter. However, some Satanists do believe in reincarnation.

Church of Satan members generally do not meet in covens as witches do, but rather in grottos. They also have their own magazines such as *The Black Flame*, *The Raven* and *The Cloven Hoof*, the official publication of the Church of Satan.

Statements of Belief

LaVey listed nine satanic statements of belief in *The Satanic Bible*, which was first published in 1969. This list codified the belief system used by many who would call themselves Satanists. A small pamphlet titled *The Safety Awareness Guide*, put out by the National Criminal Justice Center claims that *The Satanic Bible* outsold the Holy Bible on college campuses in 1988 by 10 to 1.

The nine Satanic statements are

1. Satan represents indulgence, instead of abstinence!
2. Satan represents vital existence, instead of spiritual pipe dreams!
3. Satan represents undefiled wisdom, instead of hypocritical self-deceit!

4. Satan represents kindness to those who deserve it, instead of love wasted on ingrates!

5. Satan represents vengeance, instead of turning the other cheek!

6. Satan represents responsibility to the responsible, instead of concern for psychic vampires!

7. Satan represents man as just another animal, sometimes better, more often worse than those that walk on all-fours, who, because of his "divine spiritual and intellectual development," has become the most vicious animal of all!

8. Satan represents all of the so-called sins, as they all lead to physical, mental, or emotional gratification!

9. Satan has been the best friend the church has ever had, as he has kept it in business all these years![7]

In addition to these nine statements, LaVey writes such things as "I dip my forefinger in the watery blood of your impotent mad redeemer, and write over this thorn-torn brow: The TRUE prince of evil—the king of the slaves!" Later he adds, "I gaze into the glassy eye of your fearsome Jehovah, and pluck him by the beard; I uplift a broad-axe, and split open his worm-eaten skull!"[8]

A motto in his writing says, "If a man smite thee on one cheek, smash him on the other!"[9]

Satanic writings, specifically on websites, maintain that Satanists do not approve of the use of drugs or the sacrifice of children or sacrificing animals. According to The Satanic Bible, a Satanist would only perform a human sacrifice to release a magician's wrath or to dispose of a totally obnoxious and deserving individual.[10] Even though the organization does not condone sacrifices, some who call themselves Satanists or who have adopted Satanist tenets become violent. For evidence of this, we do not need to look any further than Mark Kilroy and Steven Newberry.

Satanic Rituals

In addition to writing *The Satanic Bible*, LaVey also wrote *The Satanic Rituals*, which was released in 1972. Satanic rituals are a blend of Gnostic, Cabbalistic, Hermetic and Masonic elements.[11]

The language used in the rituals is Enochian. This is supposed to be a magical language and is thought to be older than Sanskrit. There are three kinds of rituals described in *The Satanic Bible*: the sex ritual, the compassionate ritual and the destruction ritual.

The sex ritual is most commonly known as a love charm, or spell. A person casts this spell when he wants a new lover or to increase sexual desire. These rituals should not be taken lightly. I know of pastors in South America who have easily dismissed such spells but then fallen into sexual sin. One pastor, upon obtaining a vial of love potion, mockingly spread it on himself, only to later commit adultery.

Hunting Souls

The Bible tells us of women who "hunt souls" with magic charms (see Ezek. 13:18-20). While this is the only reference in Scripture that specifically addressed hunting for souls with charms, the warning against it comes directly from God. Furthermore, it falls in line with other occult activities the Bible has warned against. Because God used such powerful words to condemn these soul-hunting charms and cautioned that anyone disobeying His words might not live to see another day, I am convinced that we should take this passage in Ezekiel very seriously.

A friend told me a story of a Satanist whom she led to the Lord. He began to weep after his conversion and confessed that he had planted fetishes with spells in them in the yards of churches. His intent was to cause the pastors to fall into sexual sin.

These fetishes will sometimes be made with graveyard dirt, urine and hair from private parts of the body. My friend went with him to dig up what he had planted. In each case, the pastor had indeed fallen into sexual sin.

Pray for Pastors

We all need to pray for our pastors on a regular basis, specifically asking God to protect them from sex spells. A spell alone will not make a godly man tumble; however, a fetish such as the ones the former Satanists had planted will activate the demonic realm. If the pastor, or any man for that matter, has given the devil a portal of entry into his life, specifically through unrepentant sin, then these wicked forces have greater power to bring on havoc, temptation and confusion.

WHILE SATAN IS NOT OMNIPRESENT OR ALL-KNOWING, HE DOES SEE PAST WRONGDOINGS AND HE KNOWS A PERSON'S WEAKNESSES.

While Satan is not omnipresent or all-knowing, he does see past wrongdoings and he knows a person's weaknesses. This is logical because those very deficiencies are the places where Satan gains footholds into a person's life. For example, if a man visits a pornographic site on the Internet, thus committing a sin, Satan will know and his demonic collaborators will target that man.

The man's weaknesses will probably be unknown to the Satanist, but they will be known to the demons who influence that Satanist. Therefore, when the Satanist plants a fetish in this man's yard, it will not be surprising if he falls into further sexual sin. The man is still the one who makes the choice to disobey God and follow the desires of his flesh. There is no "the devil made me do it" excuse that releases responsibility for our actions. Sin is sin. But the demonic powers behind a fetish can have an impact when we open the door through other sins.

Targeting Men

LaVey's daughter, Zeena, wrote the introduction for his book *The Satanic Witch*. In this book, witches are told how to sexually entrap men. Only a person who has submitted themselves to the control of perverse sexual demons could write such filth. Incidentally, Zeena later disowned her father and claimed she put a curse of death upon him.

In chapter 10, I will deal more with the way that leaders or anyone else can know if they are cursed and what to do about it.

More Curses

The compassion ritual is done to either help someone else or yourself in areas of finances, work, health, school or anything else where a person would want to succeed.

The destruction ritual is used from a base of hate and is known as a curse, hex or destroying agent.[12] LaVey added this note to the section on the destruction ritual:

> Be certain you do not care if the intended victim lives or dies, before you throw your curse, and having caused their destruction, revel, rather than feel remorse.[13]

These destructive curses have actually caused the deaths of some people. You might say that people are literally hated to death, except that we know the cursing takes place in the spiritual realm and is all too serious. We believers should not be afraid of this, rather we should be able to discern when a destructive curse has been sent against us. Sometimes there are sicknesses that we take to be simply a matter of natural course; however, they can be energized by a curse.

According to John and Paula Sandford of Elijah House, Satanists sometimes use sorcery in curses against the Church. The Sandfords, who have interviewed former Satanists and done exhaustive research in this area, provide us with the details:

> They "pray" in chants and rhythms to cause unaccount-
> able mechanical breakdowns, temper flare-ups, gossip-
> ing, adultery, etc. It may seem something too far out to
> believe that men and women in the twentieth century
> [and now the twenty-first century] can engage in such
> evil, seemingly superstitious activities, much less be
> effective in it, but Paula and I have been in direct prayer
> warfare against witches' covens and warlocks and we
> know by experience the kinds of things which can hap-
> pen. During one such battle, Paula was pregnant with
> Andrea. An unseen powerful force pushed her so strong-
> ly that she almost tumbled down the stairs. It was not
> imagination. It was an actual attempt to harm her.[14]

LaVey's Legacy

LaVey died on October 29, 1997, of heart-related problems. Blanche Barton, his long-time companion, became high priest-ess, and Peter Gilmore is now identified as high priest. The organization, which subsequently moved out of its famous all-black house headquarters in San Francisco, now lists a San Diego post-office box as its mailing address. But it retains a strong presence in Northern California. LaVey's oldest daughter, Karla, founded the First Satanic Church on October 31, 1999, in San Francisco. Zeena, who had been in a satanic baptism as a child, operates an occult bookstore in Los Angeles.

It is eye-opening to note that upon LaVey's death, Barton admitted to the *San Francisco Chronicle* that LaVey did believe in a literal Satan and the power of curses.

> "He did believe in the devil," insisted Barton, a blonde who is the mother LaVey's four-year-old son, Xerxes. "He believed in magic. He practiced it religiously." At this point Karla [LaVey's daughter] injected: "He didn't believe in a devil with horns and tails."
>
> Details of exactly how LaVey practiced his magic were a bit sketchy. In a 1967 interview, for example, LaVey told a reporter he placed a small curse on the Sutro Baths [in San Francisco] and "36 hours later it burned down." [The baths burned down in 1966.]
>
> So was he doing these sorts of hexes in more recent times, Karla was asked. "They were more personal in nature," she responded enigmatically. "And they were always deserved."[15]

Hell Fire Club

A forerunner of the Church of Satan was the Hell Fire Club, which thrived around the time of the American Revolution. The most famous of the Hell Fire Clubs was founded by the English baronet Sir Francis Dashwood. Benjamin Franklin visited the Hell Fire Club while in England. It is not clear whether he participated in the rituals or was there only to gain political influence. Numbered among its members were the British prime minister, the chancellor of the exchequer, the Lord Mayor of London, the Prince of Wales and other notables. The association itself was dedicated to "Black Magic, sexual orgies and political conspiracies."[16]

During its sexual orgies, Hell Fire Club members mocked Roman Catholics. Hell Fire Club practices drew from freemasonry. However, members were probably influenced most by the Illuminati. The Illuminati was founded by Adam Weisphaupt in Germany in the 1700s. Weisphaupt was linked to a political revolution and his group used occult practices. The organization urged initiates to assassinate princes and to influence men of status by seducing leaders and winning their confidence.[17]

The Black Mass

The Illuminati was infamous for its black mass, a form of which was performed by French nobility and can be traced back to the fifteenth century. A man named Gilles de Rais was discovered to have kidnapped, tortured and murdered children in horrid fashion, sometimes as part of the performance of the black mass.

All candidates for the Illuminati initiation were led through a long, dark tunnel into a vestibule adorned with black drapes and genuine corpses wrapped in shrouds.[18] The black mass was meant to put the flesh on an equal plane with the spirit through lust with self-denial.

The Black Arts

The lineup of people whose thinking was at least partially syncretized in LaVey's writings include Alistair Crowley and others I have already noted. The Ordo Templi Orientis (O.T.O.) was founded by Crowley. It is known to have hundreds of temples across the United States where black magic may be practiced, according to the National Criminal Justice Center.

The Process Church of The Final Judgement is, in my opinion, one of the deadliest cults in existence. It was founded in England in 1963. Members believe that killing in the name of

Satan is actually killing for Christ. Ironically, they also believe in the God of the Bible. Their teaching most likely affected other dangerous cults such as Charles Manson's "family" and was suspected to have had a role in the infamous "Son of Sam" killings in New York.

There are other more recently formed groups which practice black magic, such as The Temple of Set that was founded in San Francisco by Michael Aquino. The Temple teaches that Satan is a literal figure and contends that LaVey's form of Satanism is watered down. The Temple's teachings are drawn from German witchcraft and the black arts used by the Third Reich.

Protection from Spirits

Santeria and Palo Mayombe Aztec-Mayan magic use black pots filled with body parts, blood, coins and other items. Some Central and South American drug-running cartels follow their teaching "for protection." The Devil Ranch ring that killed Mark Kilroy was one such group

Some people would claim that Santeria, which uses either a chicken or goat for a blood sacrifice, is not black magic but white magic. It can be either. However, Palo is black magic with roots in the Aztec-Mayan culture.

Santeria originated in Nigeria and was exported to Cuba during the terrible times of slavery. It is mixed with Catholicism. There are no absolutes in Santeria. A hypothetical case in a book on Santeria illustrates their beliefs:

A Roman Catholic priest in a small Latin American town cuts down a tree to which local santeros give offerings. The priest feels he is helping his neighbors by eliminating a temptation to practice idolatry, a mortal sin. The santeros, however, feel that the Catholic priest has caused a very serious imbalance (or ashe). One santero consults an oracle, which indicates that the Catholic priest will suffer the consequences of having caused this imbalance. That night, the priest suffers a heart attack and dies. Christians denounce the santeros as belonging to a satanic cult that used black magic to harm a saintly man.[19]

When there are no absolutes and no evil, followers are not bound by any morals. This is the makeup of many of the black-magic religions.

African Roots

Many occult religions, such as Macumba, Umbanda, Santeria and voodoo, have African roots. This is not a prejudicial statement but a historical fact. We should not accept any form of occult activity simply because of the culture to which it has attached itself. If you have read this book carefully, you have noticed that Satan has attacked every region of the world and every people group. No one has escaped his attempts to draw us into one form of wickedness or another.

Macumba

Macumba, which is an umbrella term that covers many similar religions, is sorcery that can be found across South America, although it is strongest in Brazil. It is a mixture of African religion and spiritism. While there are various forms of Macumba, the spells are very strong and evil. They evoke "spirits from hell," some people who practice a related South American religion called Umbanda say. The black magic found in Macumba is clearly a form of the occult and not simply primitive people scaring others through superstition. I have encountered this black magic in Argentina.

While sharing its African roots with Macumba, most forms of Umbanda would be considered white magic. Of course, as I have pointed out already, the color of the magic does not make it any less sinful. Both are part of the occult.

Necronomicon

Another source of the darkest black magic is the book *Necronomicon*. It contains Sumarian rituals and curses that open the doors to principalities. It is said that there are gates into the earth that these incantations open which will release demons. Even people who are deep into black magic warn against using these in a casual way. Necronomicon legend tells of the author and others who have dabbled with its curses being torn to pieces. The shooters at Columbine are purported to have read this book.

Nietzsche

Nietzsche is a writer of philosophy whom young people like the Columbine shooters are reading. His teachings open people to occult thinking. For an eyes-wide-open experience, go into almost any secular bookstore and browse through his writings. Here is a quote from his prolific work:

> God is dead. But God is dead like a *vampire* who feeds on the blood of the living. God is dead, but there may still be caves for thousands of years in which his shadow will be shown. These shadows of God darken our minds. Yet they are only the ghostly shadows cast by our own fearful self-delusions[20] (emphasis added).

SATANIC RITUAL ABUSE

In the late 1980s, the media was ablaze with reports of thousands of children dying or being physically harmed at the hands of Satanists. The scare was punctuated by gruesome testimonies from victims and harrowing statistics. There was even a seminar circuit set up to help parents know how to keep their children out of harm's way. These crimes against children were given the name "Satanic Ritual Abuse" (SRA) because they often occurred during dark occult ceremonies.

Satan's schemes were finally being revealed and the whole world was paying attention. But the devil would not stand for that. A backlash emerged as government officials and journalists challenged the figures that had been quoted. In 1992, the FBI added to the confusion over SRA, releasing *Lanning's Guide to Allegations of Childhood Ritual Abuse*. The report admits that it is "certainly within the realm of possibility" that "a few cunning, secretive individuals" are killing people as part of a satanic ritual.[21] However, Lanning dismissed the idea that "thousands of offenders are abusing and even murdering tens of thousands of people as part of organized Satanic cults."[22] Lanning's report cites a lack of dead bodies and of mass graves as the reason for its conclusions.

> THE SIMPLE TRUTH IS THAT CHILDREN ARE BEING ABUSED AND MURDERED AS PART OF SATANIC RITUALS. EVEN ONE WOULD BE TOO MANY, BUT THERE ARE MANY MORE.

The FBI report may be correct about the number of victims being overblown, but this does not diminish the seriousness of the problem. The simple truth is that children are being abused and murdered as part of satanic rituals. Even one would be too many, but there are many more.

"Throughout the Western world, increasing numbers of therapists and other helping professionals are hearing accounts from children as young as two and adults ranging into the ninth decade of their lives who describe mind-numbing accounts of abuses consisting of sexual sadism and pornography, physical torture and highly sophisticated psychological manipulation," psychologist Catherine Gould wrote in the *Journal of Psychohistory*.[23]

Today counselors such as Dr. Gould are dealing with the victims who have survived SRA. JUSTUS Unlimited, a non-profit organization in Denver, Colorado, has reported getting more than 7,000 SRA-related calls a year.[24] And newspapers across the United States have carried articles about some who have died. In February of 1992, *Newsday* reported the death of a female victim:

> Members of a cult here [New York] killed ballerina Monika Beerle in August 1989 and then dismembered her and fed her flesh to the homeless as part of a Satanic ritual, law enforcement sources said yesterday after arresting a cult member in connection with the slaying.[25]

Human Sacrifice

Church of Satan leaders say that no card-carrying Satanist (this would be the red card that you receive as member for $100) would kill babies, yet some writings from religious Satanists admit there is human sacrifice! One self-defined brotherhood of Satanists, who are not affiliated with the Church of Satan, carries this statement on its website: "We play no games and with Satan it is real . . . We don't claim there is no abuse in Satanism, or human sacrifice, we believe it is up to each coven or occultic group."[26]

This website, one of the darkest ever created, actually provides a death spell that comes with this warning: "We have some spells here that are the darkest of magick. If you decide to do these, ask yourself if you really want to do them before trying.

You see, we do these for the pure pleasure of killing someone with magick."[27] Whew! Isn't cursing someone to death with the belief it will actually happen just as bad as pulling the trigger on a gun and actually committing the murder? Jesus said that if we commit adultery in our minds then we have committed it in deed.

Of course, as I pointed out earlier, as Christians we can be protected by God from these curses. Furthermore, such a curse is not guaranteed to have any effect, even for the Satanist. The unreliability of the devil is part of his nature.

Proper Counseling

I have had many calls from people who have become caught up with a former SRA victim who does not really want to be healed. This type of victim totally consumes their friends' lives. My advice to anyone encountering such an SRA victim is pray and ask God to lead you to those who can give the victim professional help.

John and Paula Sandford's son, Loren, is the pastor of New Song Fellowship in the Denver area. For a season, he and the members of his church ministered extensively to those with disassociative disorder (also called multiple-personality disorder). They were mostly SRA victims. However, as their efforts increased, the ministry began to consume all of his time and interfere with the life of the church itself. He now feels that the local congregation must not try to administer therapy to people who are SRA victims. Invariably, the churches that do are sucked in and seriously damaged. I know of some that have been shattered.

This is not to say that churches should close down their counseling centers. However, I believe that God has called and anointed certain leaders such as James G. Freisen to start and lead counseling ministries for SRA victims. We need more people trained to do this type of work, and we need halfway houses to help so that SRA victims can further their recovery in a safe environment.

The Road to Recovery

In his book *Uncovering the Mystery of MPD*, Freisen gives first-hand accounts of people he has counseled who are SRA victims. He also has seen victims who have been able to recover and live successful, productive lives after therapy. One such account is of a woman who started having memories of her parents giving her to Satan at age 6. She had also been raped and later her baby was sacrificed.[28]

Counselors such as Freisen tell me that when they first meet a woman who says she has been a victim of a satanic ritual crime, they ask her to go to a doctor to see if she has ever had a child. It is common for victims to claim a child has been taken from them. One leader told me that a very wounded woman he was counseling went to a doctor, got an examination and discovered she had never been pregnant! Of course, this is not meant in any way to take away from the truthfulness of those who have truly been abused by having a child stolen from them or a pregnancy terminated.

Face the Facts

Despite the facts, not many people are ready to deal with SRA. Victims need to be helped by trained counselors. I have heard it suggested that any Christian should be willing to open up his private home to minister to these victims! While I agree we should be willing to help them escape, great discernment needs to take place as to whether or not they really want help.

I have heard many stories about pastors who have had Satanists feign salvation experiences in order to infiltrate a church. These Satanists will also sneak into prayer groups and pretend to be extremely prophetic. In this day we need to ask for the gift of discerning of spirits to operate in our lives greater than ever before!

An excellent source for information on Satanism and SRA is Johanna Michaelsen's *Like Lambs to the Slaughter*.[29]

There are so many dangers and snares for our children today through Satanism and black magic that I feel compelled to provide a sampling of occult symbols. I have provided these in an appendix in the back of this book. Every believer needs to be aware of this evil's encroachment into society and to be able to identify it for what it is. We need to know that there really is not such a thing as white magic and black magic; it is all evil and demonically inspired. People who have practiced black magic scoff at the idea of a difference between the two. "Magic is magic," they say.

PRAYER OF PROTECTION

I am aware that some material written in this chapter is shocking to anyone who has not known the facts about black magic. It is true that we should not take on things that are greater than our understanding and should always move in wisdom. But we do not need to be afraid of these things.

Some writers have scared Christians away from confronting the enemy. They do not understand the authority they have in Jesus Christ and that Satan is already defeated. We need balance. If we use wisdom and proper prayer coverage, there is no reason to be afraid of Satan and his plots.

I am including a prayer for you to say to cleanse yourself from any defilement that may have come to you while reading this chapter:

Father God, I thank You for the Blood of the Lamb that cleanses me from all unrighteousness. I ask for cleansing now from anything unholy and/or demonic that would try to assault me as a result of reading this chapter. I bind you, Satan, from causing any backlash to me, my family or possessions in the name of Jesus Christ of Nazareth. Thank You, Lord, that Your name is above every name both in heaven and Earth. In the name of Jesus Christ, Amen.

Notes

1. "Matamoros slaying still fuels parents' anti-drug effort," *Rickross.com*, quoting the *Dallas Morning News*, April 11, 1999. http://www.rickross.com/reference/satanism49.html (accessed July 3, 2001).
2. Ibid.
3. Carl A Raschke, *Painted Black* (New York: Harper and Row, 1990), pp. 42-43.
4. Ibid., p. 53.
5. Anton LaVey, *The Satanic Bible* (New York: Avon Books, 1969), p. 4.
6. Ibid.
7. Joe Evans, *Satanism in America* (Crockett, TX: Michael Paul and Associates, n.d.), p. 7.
8. LaVey, *The Satanic Bible*, p. 30.
9. Ibid., p. 47.
10. Ibid., p. 88.
11. Anton LaVey, *The Satanic Rituals* (New York: Avon Books, 1972), p. 21.
12. LaVey, *The Satanic Bible*, p. 115.
13. Ibid., p. 118.
14. John and Paula Sandford, *Healing the Wounded Spirit* (Tulsa, OK: Victory House, 1985), pp. 283-284.
15. Susan Sward, "Satanist's Daughter to Keep the 'Faith,'" San Francisco Chronicle, November 8, 1997, p. A22.
16. Raschke, p. 84.
17. Ibid., p. 85.
18. Ibid., p. 86.
19. Raul Canizares, *Cuban Santeria* (Rochester, VT: Destiny Books, 1993), p. 5.
20. Eric Steinhart, *On Nietzsche* (Ft. Worth, TX: Wadsworth, 2000), pp. 2-3. What is so frightening about this book is that it is part of a series of books on philosophers that is packaged for universities. I bought it in a bookstore near a local college.

21. Kenneth Lanning, "Lanning's Guide to Allegations of Childhood Ritual Abuse," (Washington, DC: The Federal Bureau of Investigation, 1992), part 1, p. 1.

22. Ibid.

23. Catherine Gould, "Denying Ritual Abuse of Children," *The Journal of Psychohistory*, Vol. 22, 1995.

24. Daniel Ryder, *Cover-Up of the Century: Satanic Ritual Crime and Conspiracy*.

25. *Newsday*, February 18, 1992.

26. I am not providing the actual name of this group or the website, although it was accessed on July 13, 2001 to obtain this quote. This is a dark occult website that no one should visit.

27. Ibid.

28. James Freisen, *Uncovering the Mystery of MPD* (San Bernadino, CA: Here's Life Publishers, 1991), p. 81.

29. Johanna Michaelsen, *Like Lambs to the Slaughter* (Eugene, OR: Harvest House, 1989).

CHAPTER 8

PROTECTING
YOUR FAMILY
FROM THE
OCCULT

I have written this book in such bold detail to get your attention. Are your eyes wide open yet? If you have caught my message, then by now you know that the occult and all of its variations are being mainstreamed into our society, with our children as prime targets. As I have traveled around the world, I have seen firsthand that this is true not just in the United States, but in Europe, Latin America, Asia, Africa—everywhere I go.

If you are like me, then right about now you are asking: *How can I protect my family? What do I do to keep the occult from influencing my children? Can I do anything more than pray?*

Of course, you need to break any ties you, your family or your ancestors have had with the occult. As I have already mentioned, we will deal with this in chapters 9 and 10.

There are also ways to protect your family. One of the best actions a parent can take is to watch for signs that your children are involved in any of the activities warned against in this book and to understand how deep into the occult that child has or has not gone.

LEVELS OF OCCULT INVOLVEMENT

In order to fully understand the occult and its threat to our families, it is important to realize that there are various levels of occult involvement.[1] Drawing upon information from the National Criminal Justice Task Force, the book *Painted Black*, personal interviews with people who have come out of the occult and other resources, I have broken down occult involvement into various stages. While involvement at any level is a sin, obviously the deeper a person goes, the greater the spiritual damage. Understanding these tiers of involvement will help us recognize and deal with the occult and the people involved in it.

Thrill Seekers

This is a fairly innocent level of involvement. It can include astrological forecasts, tea-leaf reading, Ouija boards, horror movies and some superstition. The people participating in such activities usually do not realize that they are really involving themselves in the occult. In fact, many are often surprised when they are told that they have been involved in dangerous practices.

I find that almost everyone, by the time he or she has reached adulthood, has in some way participated in or at least been exposed to one occult practice or another. This may have happened when the person read his or her horoscope in a newspaper, when they had their palms read at a carnival or when they watched a movie such as *Dracula*.

On the Fringe

Fringe-level involvement edges a person closer to seriously and deliberately practicing the occult. Some fringe activities bleed between the levels. The difference is in the intention of the practitioner. For instance, those playing Magic: The Gathering may or may not realize that it is an occult game. It is understandable that some who do not have a clear understanding of what the occult is might see Magic: The Gathering as mere fantasy and entertainment. On the other hand, those who have already been involved in the occult at any level will be drawn to the game just as Wiccans are drawn to *Harry Potter*. A person who has experimented with sorcery, mind control or other kinds of divination will see similar practices in Magic: The Gathering and other games.

It is easy for a thrill seeker to move to the fringe. The person who, on the more innocent level, occasionally glanced at an astrological chart, will start reading his or her horoscope on a regular basis. Likewise, listening to heavy metal music can also pull a person deeper into occult involvement. The pop singer Eminem has received several music awards even though his songs glamorize rape and murder. Such widespread acceptance of this kind of music shows that as a society we do not recognize how breaking down moral standards makes us more susceptible to occult practice.

Another type of fringe-level involvement is tarot-card reading. A group may decide to go to a palm reader for kicks. Usually palm readers also have tarot cards. Some who have their palms read will be looking for more than a thrill. They may actually start to desire to have not only their fortunes told, but they will also want to know how to use the tarot cards.

When a person reaches the fringe level, he or she usually starts experimenting with drugs and immoral sex—often this happens at parties. Former occultists tell me that those who are seriously into the occult offer newcomers drugs or alcohol, get them high and lead them into sexual activities with the intent of winning their confidence and eventually leading them further into the occult. These occultists will sometimes take a newcomer's picture and later use it for blackmail if he or she does not come to occult meetings or get involved on a deeper level.

Some people who end up in the occult start out by reading books such as *Necronomicon* or the writings of Nietzsche. A few will pick up *The Satanic Bible* out of fascination. I had a friend in college who read *The Satanic Bible*. It confused him and caused him to doubt his salvation.

Role-playing game participants may start out as thrill seekers, but very quickly they progress to the fringe level and beyond. Sean Sellers is the young man who brutally killed both of his parents. He had been a Dungeons and Dragons player. I believe there was a connection between the role-playing game and his heinous criminal acts. Sellers, like most players, was sucked into the excitement, energy

> DABBLERS ARE MUCH MORE INTENTIONAL IN THEIR OCCULT INVOLVEMENT. THEY MAY USE DRUGS MORE, READ BOOKS ON SATANISM ON A REGULAR BASIS OR PARTICIPATE IN IMMORAL SEXUAL PRACTICES.

and challenge of the game. As he thrust himself into Dungeons and Dragons, it consumed him and captured his imagination. He then took the violence found in this fantasy game and crossed over the line into the real world. For Sean, the fantasy world of Dungeons and Dragons became his reality and he acted upon it. That game in particular can quickly suck its players into the occult at a very deep level.

Dabblers

Dabblers are much more intentional in their occult involvement. They may use drugs more, read books on Satanism on a regular basis or participate in immoral sexual practices.

For many young people, this level of occult involvement seems exciting and offers them power. So many are looking for meaning in their lives; some feel out of control. They think that the rituals of Satanism or witchcraft will put them in the driver's seat. They believe these practices allow them to take charge of their lives, even to hurt people who have hurt them. They see that they can cast a positive spell to help them complete their homework or a destructive curse to "punish" an unsympathetic boss. From this point, they not only dabble, but begin to form a belief system with the occult at its core. This often marks a drastic departure from the morals with which they have been raised.

The Sophisticated Level

At this juncture, dabblers choose which direction they want to take into the intentional, purposeful practice of the occult. Some will move deeper into a sophisticated level of white magic. Others take up the practice of Satanism or black magic. As I pointed out in the chapter 4, Wiccans tend to practice white magic and claim that they do not cast harmful spells. Many who first learned about sorcery from *Harry Potter* and other popular books take this path. No wonder Wicca has seen such a revival! Those who take the black-magic route sometimes associate themselves with the Church of Satan or some other dark occult group. Others are self-styled in their approaches and often mix white and black magic.

Self-Styled Occultists

The people who participate on this level are not generally a part of an organized cult, such as the Temple of Set or the Church of

Satan. They are usually self-taught and eclectic in their occult belief system. This is the level on which Pete Roland, whom I wrote about in chapter 7, operated. While not all self-styled occultists become murderers, many such as Roland do eventually commit violent acts.

On this level, usually a couple of friends develop what they believe. One, who has studied on his own, is the ringleader and begins to teach others. This level is extremely dangerous as those involved often incorporate drugs, heavy-metal music and role-playing games into their own religion. As a result, fantasy can become reality and people can live it out by doing brutal acts such as killing animals or people.

Since this is self-styled, occultists at this level use either white or black magic and sometimes combine the two.

The Serious Level

People on the serious level are usually part of an organized group. They have progressed through the previous levels, although there is no set route. Some may have joined with Wiccans for a time, others may have read Anton LaVey's works and tried their hand at spellcasting. While the dabbler previously advanced to the sophisticated level when he made a choice about his general direction in the occult, it is at the serious level that he fully immerses himself into the practice of one or more of the branches of the occult.

Whereas people at the other levels may or may not attempt to be secretive about their participation in the occult, when they reach this level it usually requires secrecy.

It would be a mistake to think that these people are simply the dregs of society—not so! You would be shocked to know who they are. They are teachers, lawyers, landlords and bankers. They also are medical doctors and nurses. Most of them go about their business in a professional manner. But some have used their positions of power to further their demonic religion. In fact, while it is thankfully still a rare occurrence, I have friends who have been assaulted by Satanists.

In one instance, a Christian who was hospitalized after having a stroke nearly died. The Lord spoke to an intercessor, telling him to go to the hospital because the Christian was under satanic attack. When the intercessor arrived, his friend was unattended and bleeding to death. Two intravenous needles had been inserted into the hospitalized man's body, one in each arm. One contained what turned out to be an overdose of blood thinner. The other appeared to have been forced out of place, and blood was spewing out of the patient's arm. The intercessor was able to correct the situation and save the man's life. In was later learned that the patient had seen an hospital attendant wearing an occult ring that bore a goat's head. While they were not able to prove the attendant had caused the problem, in the spirit they felt certain there was a connection.

It is always important to be alert when we have a loved one in the hospital—not afraid or paranoid, just alert. There are occultists who work in medical facilities and, on occasion, they will use their position to advance the demonic cause. However, we should remember that God is the great physician who can and does heal through miracles and through skilled medical professionals.

It is critical to understand that those who reach the serious level are dedicated. Some people who participate in Satanism consider committed Christians a threat. The following are some of the groups and practices that are on the serious level:

1. Church of Satan
2. Temple of Set
3. Wicca
4. Santeria

The Criminal Level

The last and darkest of these degrees of involvement is the criminal level. Many law-enforcement officers in virtually every state in America know about this level. At this level, occultists do not want to be discovered and they attempt to cover their tracks.

Of course, God can discover and uncover anything, as we pray. In a conversation with an ex-Satanist who is now a committed Christian, I received some intriguing information. He said to me:

> You know, you intercessors really have the right idea when you strategically study an area. When I was a Satanist, [whether he was self-styled, a member of the Church of Satan or a member of some other group, he did not say] we would target different areas and then draw a circle around the circumference to begin to infiltrate it.
>
> One of the things we would do was to get on school grounds and plant a fetish to start cursing the school. Then we would hang around on the outside of the school grounds and give the kids candy and drugs to lure them into the occult.[2]

We need to pray for our schools and our children to protect them from satanic activity. While it is a given, this is just another reason to teach children to never talk with or take anything from a stranger.

OCCULT RITUALS

One of the crimes some occultists commit is the blood sacrifice. Serious black-magic practitioners say a curse sent through a blood sacrifice is very strong, with a human sacrifice being the strongest. If a human sacrifice has been made, it may require fasting to break its effect. In his book *The Black Arts*, Richard Cavandish mentions two main reasons for a literal sacrifice:

1. *To provide energy.* Blood is considered to be the source of live energy and it is released in the sacrifice.
2. *To give a psychological charge or kick to the participants.* Cavandish, a leading author of occult traditions, maintains that this is the most important reason for the sacrifice.[3]

I am going to add a third to this list:

3. *To empower the curse, releasing a high-level demon to see that the curse comes to pass.* This can be a spirit of death, a spirit of destruction or another powerful demon. Satanists sometimes call this being hated to death.

Typical crime-scene clues that are unique to Satanism and witchcraft that police might look for in order to recognize an occult crime include the following:

1. the mockery of Christianity in symbols and liturgy;
2. inverted crosses;
3. stolen Christian artifacts;
4. black candles;
5. bent or broken crosses (used as peace symbols);
6. drawings, graffiti on walls and streets;
7. pentagrams drawn on walls or floors (sometimes in blood);
8. goats' heads worn as a sign of allegiance to Satan;
9. nondiscernible alphabets or scrawlings;
10. grave robbings;

11. animal mutilations (removal of blood and body parts);
12. missing body parts;
13. unusual tattoos, cuts, slash marks and body marks [on suspects];
14. bloodletting.[4]

A Serious Warning

What I am going to share with you next is very important. Please take note of this section. If you come across a Satanic altar as you are prayer walking or in some other situation, *do not* attempt to kick it over without proper prayer backing. Powerful curses have been released on these altars. They can and do affect those who presumptuously destroy them. While we have authority over every evil thing (see Luke 10:19), we might have a hole in our armor (areas of secret sin or woundedness) which may allow the curse to have an effect.

I have known intercessors who moved in presumption and then saw their families fall apart, got divorced or were financially ruined. If you come across a Satanic ritualistic area, ask the Lord to protect you. Then find someone who knows what they are doing and get proper prayer backup before destroying the altar. If the altar has blood or other signs of possible criminal activity, I suggest you call the police to report its location.

It is shocking how criminal occult elements have used children while their parents thought they were playing and learning. The socioeconomic status or race of the child does not seem to matter. I know of specific incidents in which little children have been abducted during preschool and then used in occult rituals. The book *Painted Black* provides more details on this type of tragedy.

Being Watchful

Here are some warning signs. If you detect any of them in your children, it does not necessarily mean they are being used in occult rituals, but you should investigate and determine the cause.

1. Preoccupation with urine and feces, such as smearing feces in the bathroom.
2. Aggressive or violent play with sadistic qualities such as mutilation of animals.
3. Bleeding around the rectum, fear of anyone looking while he or she uses the bathroom and/or hiding his or her private parts.
4. References to "my other mommy or daddy."
5. Preoccupation with the devil or magic.
6. Fear of being restrained.
7. Nightmares or dreams about being hurt or with strange themes too mature for a small child to understand.
8. Mention of "bad people" hurting his or her parents.[5]

It is vitally important that you believe your children if they tell you any of the things on this list. If you suspect sexual molestation, take your child to the doctor. Also, if he is afraid of going to preschool or to a babysitter, ask him why he does not want to go. Do not just discount what he says.

I have friends whose children were satanically abused and it has taken them years of work to get their children free from outbursts of wrath, cursing, and sexually explicit language. My friends never suspected their kindly neighbors whom they thought of as "grandma and grandpa."

From this experience I have learned to use great discernment. We are to love our neighbors, but that does not mean we give them carte blanche with our kids. As parents, we need to exercise full diligence. We ought to talk to the parents of our children's friends. Find out who the primary caregiver is. But do not stop there. Ask about every person in the family who might be in the house when your child is there.

Find out what your children will be doing while visiting their friend's house. What will be on television? Will there be video games? Which ones? Ask specifically about Pokemon and *Harry Potter*. Make it clear you do not want your children involved with either one of

> DO NOT GET
> HYSTERICAL
> BECAUSE YOUR
> CHILD WANTS TO
> WEAR ALL BLACK.
> I WEAR BLACK AND
> I AM CERTAINLY
> NOT A SATANIST.

these. Is there anything inappropriate that goes on in that house to which you do not want your children exposed? Too many parents never bother to find out about the parents or the house where their kids visit. This is a huge mistake. As good parents, we need to ask.

TELLTALE SIGNS OF OCCULT INVOLVEMENT

As a guardian over your family, it is critical that you learn to watch the children and teenagers you are raising to see if they are somehow involved in the occult. As I mentioned earlier, we are not to be ignorant of Satan's devices (see 2 Cor. 2:11).

There are warning signs that will tell you whether or not they have become involved in the occult. Before I list these warning signs, I want to give you a word of caution. Some of these signs can be related to other things or can simply indicate a pref-erence of a style of dress. Do not get hysterical because your child wants to wear all black. I wear black and I am certainly not a Satanist. Youth also may go through times of depression or reject their friends—either can be totally unrelated to being in the occult. Silver jewelry is popular today and not necessarily a sign of involvement in occult activity.

Pray for wisdom and do not instantly accuse your child of having occult involvement. If you see a number of warning signs or material that is undisputedly occult (i.e., occult markings on notebooks or a copy of *The Satanic Bible*), then you must approach them. Remember, your child may just be reading such a book just for the thrill of it. However, great wisdom needs to be shown in this area.

Here are a few of the warning signs I have adapted from Randy Skinner's *Safety Awareness Guide*.

1. Secrecy and isolation
2. Rejection of friends
3. Excessive secrecy regarding new friends and activities
4. Alienated, argumentative or violent
5. Rejection of parental values
6. Loss of humor
7. Change of school habits
8. Confused about gender
9. Fearful. (This is often happens after a person willingly or unwillingly confesses all past sins for ritual purposes of cleansing. This statement is taped and used against the person if he or she later tries to leave the group.)
10. Unreasonable feelings of paranoia directed toward authorities
11. Excessive viewing of horror movies or heavy-metal music videos, such as *The Faces of Death* and *The Believer*

12. Immoral sexual activity
13. Heavy participation in fantasy games. (Fantasy games have no rules or guidelines. They encourage creativity without boundaries. The line between reality and fantasy becomes blurred.)
14. Viewing of objectionable material on the computer, particularly visiting occult websites
15. Interest in drugs, especially hallucinogenics
16. Depressive personality
17. Draping hair across the left eye
18. Wearing pale make-up, dying hair black
19. Listening to black metal or heavy metal music groups with occult lyrics, symbols or references to occult worship
20. Fingernails painted black. Left hand nails longer than right hand nails. (The left side of body represents evil in the occult.)
21. Preoccupation with black clothing
22. Left sleeve rolled up by itself. (This is used in schools, malls and other places to signify membership in a satanic group.)
23. Greeting with left-hand horn signal (see appendix 3.)
24. Wearing only silver jewelry and refusing to wear gold jewelry. (Gold jewelry is considered a Christian metal.)
25. Phone calls asking for someone other than your child. (Caller may be asking for your child using his or her satanic name.)
26. Obsession with death
27. Writing essays and reports on death and/or the occult
28. Changes in bedroom appearance. (A bedroom changes as the child grows, but here are some things to look for: pentagrams; symbols taped or painted on floor

under the carpet or bed; hidden occult objects; the
walls painted black.)

29. Use of less electric light and more candles
30. Satanic alphabet used on notebooks
31. Writing backwards
32. Carrying a book of shadows. (This is the most impor-
    tant personal book of poetry, prose, spells, incanta-
    tions and meeting places. It is usually in a spiral
    notebook, but may have another book cover on it.)
33. Books dealing with rituals or necromancy, Satanism,
    black magic or witchcraft. (One such book is *Helter
    Skelter*.)
34. School locker contains satanic items
35. Self-mutilation or cuts on a continual basis. (Cuts
    may be on the breast, ankles or arms; needle marks
    used to drain blood for consumption; look for marks
    on left side of the body)
36. Mutilation or torture of animals[6]

In chapter 3, I gave some guidance as to what to do if you
suspect your child is into the occult. You might want to go back
and reread that section. Here are some additional tips:

1. The first thing to do if you suspect your child is in the
   occult is to pray. Ask God to reveal every hidden and
   secret thing. The following Scriptures tell us that God
   wants to reveal secret things to us:

   He reveals deep and secret things; He knows
   what is in the darkness, and light dwells with
   him (Dan. 2:22).

For nothing is secret that will not be revealed, nor anything hidden that will not be known and come to light (Luke 8:17).

2. Go through his or her room, and ask the Holy Spirit to guide you in your search. Be aware that your child will hide things, as I mentioned earlier, so be creative in your searching. Look under the mattress and in the mattress. Look in stuffed animals, behind drawers and any other place something could be hidden.

3. Check his or her notebooks. Go through them to see if they include any occult drawings.

4. Look at the words to the music your child is listening to. Heavy-metal music is a huge doorway into the occult. Is he or she listening to Black Sabbath, AC/DC, Marilyn Manson, KISS or some other heavy-metal group? There are categories of heavy metal such as black metal and death rock. Get to know the names and types and keep your children away from them.

5. Are they watching slasher videos, such as *Friday the Thirteenth, Halloween* or *Nightmare on Elm Street*?

6. Are they obsessed with fantasy role-playing games? Particularly watch for Dungeons and Dragons although I would also be wary of Magic: The Gathering.

7. Any of the other warning signs that I listed earlier in conjunction with any of these six.

Occult Symbols

I am including a section on occult symbols in appendix 3. It is a valuable tool in recognizing occult activity.

Confronting Your Child

What do you do once you are pretty sure that your child is at least dabbling in the occult? I want to quote Johanna Michaelsen here because what she says is so relevant and well put:

> Do not make the mistake of assuming that this is all just a fad or a phase that all kids go through! Of course, not every kid who gets into devil worship necessarily goes out and kills someone or commits suicide, but a growing number of them do. How many of you are willing to take that chance? Unfortunately, some parents who have seen these signs and gone to teachers or even ministers for counsel have been turned away with a patronizing pat on the head and the empty assurance that "it's just a phase that all kids go through."[7]

If you have found some occult objects in your child's room, the next step is confrontation. Be aware that your child may tell you that the material belongs to a friend who left it at the house. When this happens, it is a very good time, even if you see scant evidence or your child denies any involvement, to have a talk about the occult. Your child, if old enough, might even be willing to read some of the material in this book! But, as a parent, use some discretion.

When a Parent Did Not Act

Pete Roland, who killed a classmate in a satanic murder, had a mother who suspected something was very wrong with him. When she confronted him, he denied involvement. Here are her own words from a "Geraldo" television special.

> I feel very guilty that I didn't pay attention . . . I saw the satanic symbols in his book work and I had spoken to

him about it. It didn't mean anything, you know, it was—I assumed it was a passing phase. I had my things when I was that age; I assumed that he had his. *I assumed wrong*. I would advise anybody, if they see anything like that, to look into it, don't ignore it. It doesn't pass . . . I wish I had listened to the music, I wish I had thrown it out. I wish I had gone to school and talked to him, talked to his friends' mothers; maybe they saw some things that I didn't see. Maybe if we had put them together we could have come with something (emphasis added).[8]

Pete Roland is in prison serving a life sentence for murder. He will never get out and, barring some kind of miracle, his mother will likely never get to hold her son in her arms again.

TAKE IT TO HEART

At this point you may be saying, "Cindy, aren't you just being melodramatic?" No, a thousand times, no! If this chapter saves even one life, it will be worth the writing—all the prayer, pain, warfare—everything!

I know how easy it is to believe your child when he or she lies to you. My daughter Mary was on drugs for a short period of her life. However, every time I prayed and asked that God would uncover every secret thing she was doing, He did! She is whole and walking with the Lord today.

One of the best things you can do for your children as they are growing up is to talk with them and their friends to keep the communication lines open. At a later time, you may need to draw on the love that you have built between you and your child. Get to know your kids's friends. Have them over to your home. Build love and trust with them as well.

Mike and I found out about our daughter's involvement with drugs through her best friend, who came over one night to tell us. Afterward, Mike, Mary's brother and I sat down with Mary and her best friend. At first she vehemently denied the allegations; but, finally, as her friend encouraged her and after we assured her that we loved her, she broke down and we were able to establish some guidelines in her life to help her get free.

Maybe you have a child who has been involved in drugs or other dangerous activities. Perhaps they have been influenced by some of their friends. Even if your child has stopped seeing the friends who have been a bad influence, I encourage you to talk with other parents about the situation. Each parent needs to decide if they want their children involved.

When confronting your child, ask the Lord to show you how deep the level of involvement is. If you suspect it is on the serious or criminal level (for instance, you find a note that says he is planning to kill himself or someone else) you must take immediate action. Talk to his school counselor or ask for advice from the juvenile crimes division of your local law enforcement office. Ask if there is an officer who deals with occult crimes. After the school shootings at Columbine and other places, the police will most likely take you seriously. If you suspect your child might harm you in some way, take steps to protect yourself. One step is to remove all weapons from the house.

I do not want to be an alarmist. In fact, that is something that I have struggled with in writing this chapter; yet I want you to be safe.

Remember, as long as your children are minors and living in your house, you have a right to throw out all occult material, take down objectionable posters and clear out their rooms. If they are adults, tell them they must remove the material or move out immediately. Also, do not be afraid to tell them which friends you do not feel good about.

Remember the story about Cassie Bernall, who died a martyr's death at the Columbine shooting? Her parents applied tough love and threw away CDs and videos that encouraged violence or pertained to witchcraft and the occult. She is in heaven today because of her parents' courage.

If you do find that your son or daughter is involved in some level of occult activity, do not panic! God is fully able to help you and work a miracle in your child's life through prayer and intercession.

Notes

1. I am indebted to the National Criminal Justice Task Force's pamphlet, *Satanism in America* for the names of the different levels of occult practices. While I have my own interpretations of what some of the levels consist of, I have used their names of levels.
2. Interview with an ex-Satanist whose identity is not revealed to protect him and his family.
3. *Satanism in America*, p. 22.
4. Ibid., p. 21.
5. *Satanism in America*, p. 22, and personal knowledge.
6. Randy Skinner, *The Safety Awareness Guide* (self-published).
7. Johanna Michaelsen, *Like Lambs to the Slaughter* (Eugene, OR: Harvest House, 1989), p. 273.
8. Ibid., p. 275.

CHAPTER 9

WHAT! LITTLE OLE ME HAVE A DEMON?

I am going to keep the promise I made to you at the beginning of this book. In this chapter (and the next one which is on breaking curses) I am going to deal with the different areas in your life in which you might have a bondage from occult involvement. Have you been keeping a list as you have been reading this book? If you have, pull it out now. It not, then go ahead and start one now. Be sure to include on the list anything you have done that I have written about, including having your palm read, reading an astrological forecast and playing with a Ouiji board.

DEMONOLOGY 101

Before we address specific problems and show you how to be free from any occult experiences in your past, we must first have a basic understanding of demonology. There are many excellent books that have been written on this subject (see the recommended reading list at the back of this book), so this chapter will only be a general introduction to the subject. However, I believe it will be enough to assist you in getting free or at least point you in the right direction.

The subject of demons sounds kind of spooky to many believers. On the other hand, for those of you who have survived reading this book up to this point, including the chapter on black magic, nothing will sound too bizarre!

I did not know much about demons until I was in my thirties. I found out a little in college, but my first experiences were rather scary—mostly because I did not understand what was happening around me.

Jumping into the Fray

My first big encounter with a demonized person was wild! My nice Baptist upbringing had not prepared me for anything like what I would see. This is not in any way to put down the great truths of Scripture I was taught. My father was the pastor, and he did a great job of instilling the basics of faith in me. However, dealing with demons was not part of the teaching. Nonetheless, my mother recently informed me that my dad had actually done a deliverance and set a person free—an incident I knew nothing about!

Then, in the early 1980s, my husband, Mike, and I opened our home to a woman whose husband had tried to kill her. She was about 48 years old and, other than being quite distressed over her situation (who wouldn't be?), she seemed quite normal. One nice bright day this woman and I were standing in the kitchen when she suddenly grabbed her side and said, "Cindy, I hurt so bad!" Remember, at this time I was a mostly ignorant, never-had-cast-a-demon-out-of-anyone, young woman.

I immediately thought things such as, *Should I call a doctor* and *Maybe you should go lie down.* She went to lie down, and I decided that I would go lay hands on her. The second I approached her, her face contorted, and a masculine voice rasped out of her female mouth, "I'm going to kill her! She deserves to die! I'm going to kill you, too!"

At that point she had my full attention!

I immediately thought of my two little children who were asleep in the other room. Something rose up inside me—that protective, mother-bear type of thing. I looked right into the eye of what I now know was a demon and boldly said, "Oh, no, you are not! You are not going to kill her or me or anyone else!"

The demonic spirit that was operating through her was trying to get off the bed. Not knowing what else to do, I grabbed my Bible and sat right on top of her. This was a rather comical scene because I was a size-four, 5-foot-2-inch individual and she was a much larger person. I recalled conversations I had heard among students at the Christian college I had attended. Among the many ideas discussed was the principle that demons could not stand to hear about the Blood of Jesus. Having at least one weapon in my arsenal, I opened my Bible to several Scriptures that address the Blood (see 1 Pet. 1:2; 1 John 1:7; Heb. 10:19).

Standing My Ground

I told the demon that it could not touch us because this woman was a blood-bought child of God and so was I. The diabolical spirit hissed, "Oh, yes I have a right to her. Her family killed Indians, murdered them and threw them down a well!" This did not daunt me even though I knew absolutely nothing about generational curses at the time. Knowing that I could be in big trouble, I cried out to the Lord to send His angels to protect us. After that, I simply held my Bible and forbade that spirit in the name of Jesus from speaking or harming any of us. In a moment, I saw a change in my friend's eyes and she was back!

I must admit that I was a bit wary, so I continued to sit on top of her for a while. Finally I realized that whatever had spoken through her was no longer manifesting itself, so I slid onto the floor, completely exhausted. I knew that the demonic spirit was not gone, but everything seemed stable for now. I also realized that I was in way over my head.

When I told her what had happened, she did not remember a thing. However she did call someone else who knew about deliverance and went for help.

Later, I found out that the demon in her had thrown six men across the room during her deliverance. All I could do was say to the Lord, "Thank you, God, for sending those big angels to help me when I asked you to."

Lesson Learned

Not a very auspicious beginning, I know. The good part is that I have since learned I have authority through the name of Jesus Christ. No demon has thrown me across the floor like the ones that dealt with her—nothing even close to that has ever happened to me.

Perhaps the most important thing this experience taught me was that demons are very, very real. If I had held any doubts at all before that encounter, they were totally gone.

A Call from God

A short time later, a very reputable prophet prophesied that God was going to use me to cast out demons. Well, I was still traumatized from my first encounter with fallen angels and did not think that was good news at all!

In fact, I was so shaken that I lay in bed the next day having a huge fight with God. "Lord," I whined, "I don't want to cast out demons. Demons scare me. I don't like them. Let someone else cast them out."

God and I continued to battle over this issue for days. I tried to convince Him that I was not the person to cast out demons. Either God was not listening or He was simply chuckling. He obviously knew that not only would I some day cast demons out of people but that I would also start an international group of intercessors and teach about powers of the air and spiritual principalities. For more information on these subjects you can read my book *Possessing the Gates of the Enemy*.

One day during this wrestling time with the Lord, a friend called me and said, "Cindy, what are you doing?"

"I'm in bed," I moaned. "I've stapled the sheets over my head and I'm not coming out!"

How I thank God for being very patient with me.

I finally came out of my bedroom and began an earnest study of demonology. The Lord was gracious to lead me to tapes, books and people who really knew how to cast out demons. This chapter is full of what I have learned.

When I studied Mark 16:17, I knew I had to say yes to God. That verse reads:

And these signs will follow those who believe: In my name *they will cast out demons*; they will speak with new tongues (emphasis added).

The primary word for "believe" in the Greek language of the New Testament is *pisteuo*. It has to do with righteousness and with putting one's faith and trust in Christ for salvation. It is also the word used by Jesus to describe the faith that can move mountains (see Matt. 17:20). Mark 16:17 also uses the word: "those who believe." When I understood that the casting out of demons was the responsibility of every believer, I knew I had to walk in obedience and learn about the ministry of deliverance.

The Origin of Demons

One of the first questions I asked in my studies on demonology was "Where do *they* come from?" The Bible does not precisely tell us of their origin. But there are three main theories concerning the origin of demons:

1. The Gap Theory is described by Gordon Lindsay who wrote: "There is a general belief among Bible scholars that demons had their origin in a pre-Adamic age."[1] In this theory, the demons are not fallen angels, but the actual people who were part of this age who participated in Satan's rebellion. This rebellion of Satan occurred between Genesis 1:1 and Genesis 1:2. The premise is that God created the world in a perfect state, not the chaos as described in verse 2. Other supporting scriptures for this theory are found in Jeremiah 4:23-26, Ezekiel 28:14-15, Isaiah 14:13-14 and Isaiah 24:1.

2. Demons are the offspring of the sons of God (angels) and the daughters of men (see Gen. 6:2) who produced giants or the mighty men of old (see Gen. 6:4). These giants are called *nephilim* and had abnormal bodies. Some had six fingers (1 Chron. 20:6). This whole subject is quite fascinating. Some believe this is where the legends of Thor, Zeus and other Greek gods got their origins. These fallen angels might be described in Jude 6 as ones bound in chains who did not keep their proper domain. Other Scriptures concerning this subject include Job 1:6, 2:1 and 38:7.

3. Demons are fallen angels. This is most commonly taught theory on the origin of demons and the easiest to understand. Scriptures for this interpretation include Matthew 12:24; Revelation 12:4,7,9; Jude 6; 2 Peter 2:4.

While the Bible is unclear as to the origin of demons, it is very clear in stating that they do exist. Many deliverance teachers believe that there are at least two orders of spirits in this realm. High-level spirits or princes (see Dan. 10:13,20; Eph. 6:12) are powers such as the Demon of Persia in Daniel 10. They generally do not seek embodiment in a person, but there are exceptions. The lower order of spirits would include demons of lust, fear and other sins, and they commonly seek embodiment.

Attributes of a Demon

What are the characteristics of demons? First of all, they are spirit beings that have individual personalities. Derek Prince gives five accepted marks of their personalities:

1. **Will.** In Matthew 12:44 the demon says, "I *will* return to my house" (emphasis added).
2. **Emotion.** In James 2:19, even the demons believe—and tremble!
3. **Intellect.** In Mark 1:24, a demon speaks, "I know who You are—the Holy One of God."
4. **Self-awareness.** In Mark 5:9 the demon reveals his name: "My name is Legion; for we are many."
5. **Ability to speak.** See Mark 5:9.[2]

It does not take long in the deliverance ministry before you know that the demons have individual personalities. In fact, some demons are smarter than others. At times, some act pretty stupid.

Liar, Liar

Several years ago, during the ministry time at a retreat, I was calling spirits out of a woman. Upon addressing a spirit of abandonment, the demon spoke through her and lied, "I've already gone!" I was not fooled, and I guarantee you that he really was cast out a moment later!

You may find this hard to believe, but at times deliverance can actually be quite fun. During that deliverance at the retreat, I finally called out what I knew to be the strongman of rejection. The spirit flipped the woman over on her stomach, started kicking her feet and whined, "I'm the last one, I'm the last one." While they often lie, I knew that what the spirit had said was indeed the case and it was quickly removed.

A Counterfeit Spirit

Lower level demons generally seek embodiment. Matthew 12:43 indicates that "When an unclean spirit goes out of a man, he goes through dry places, seeking rest, and finds none." To me, the dry place is anywhere outside of the human body, because our bodies are made up of such a large percentage of water.

Demons make counterfeits of the things of God. Their ways are the opposite of the workings of the Holy Spirit. What do I mean?

When the Holy Spirit fills a person's life, He makes that person more like Himself. The fruit of the Holy Spirit will begin to manifest itself and become evident in the person. He or she will be filled with the love and mercy of God.

On the other hand, when a person is demonized, that spirit's influence begins to produce fruit of its own diabolic kind and personality. For instance, a spirit of lust will give the person lustful thoughts. That person

WHAT ARE THE CHARACTERISTICS OF DEMONS? FIRST OF ALL, THEY ARE SPIRIT BEINGS THAT HAVE INDIVIDUAL PERSONALITIES.

will desire illicit sex. The spirit of lust will emanate from that person's eyes. I, as a woman, have felt this spirit's presence manifest itself through a man many times. It does not happen because of my looks. The spirit does not care if the object of lust is 10, 30 or 83 years old! One of the primary ways you can know a spirit of lust is at work is when you see a person's eyes sweep your whole body the moment they come into contact with you. Of course, women can help discourage the spirit of lust by carefully selecting what they wear.

Christians and Demons

One of the most often asked questions is whether or not a Christian can be demon possessed. My answer is no. However, Christians can be demonized.

I use the term "demonized" because to be "possessed" indicates that the person is owned by the demon. God owns the believer; however, a Christian can be influenced by a demon, or demonized. I once heard a leader say that a Christian can have anything he wants—and that includes a demon!

Humans are made up of three parts: the spirit, the soul and the body. This is revealed in 1 Thessalonians 5:23:

> Now may the God of peace Himself sanctify you completely; and may your whole spirit, soul, and body be preserved blameless at the coming of our Lord Jesus Christ.

Our spirits, as believers, are wholly owned by God. However, our souls, or the emotional realm, and our physical bodies may be subject to demonization. For instance, our minds may be demonized by a spirit of fear or our bodies may be demonized by a spirit of infirmity. Either one could paralyze us.

How They Get In

I realize that the demonization of Christians is hard for some believers to understand, but there appears to be a biblical precedent that a born-again believer was, indeed, demonized. The Bible says that Simon the Sorcerer believed and was baptized (see Acts 8:13). However, he was still demonized and tried to buy the power of the Holy Spirit.

The Bible does not say that Simon faked his conversion, as some people might argue. Since baptism alone is not a guarantee of salvation, we really do not know the state of Simon's soul. But surely Philip would not have been a part of his water baptism if he thought Simon's conversion was not real.

Simon had three classic entry points that caused him to be demonized.

Bitterness. Bitterness and unforgiveness are two primary entry points that cause a person to be demonized. In order to receive deliverance, it is important to forgive all those who have trespassed against you and ask God to heal you from all bitterness.

Iniquity. This includes the sins of the fathers that we inherit. I am going to write about this in the next chapter on breaking curses.

The occult. Of course, this is the primary subject of this book. At the end of this chapter, I will include a cleansing prayer for you to read to renounce all occult involvement.

Simon was deeply demonized through the occult. Finis J. Dake cites ancient ecclesiastical writers who said, "Simon claimed he was the Father who gave the law of Moses; that he came in the reign of Tiberias in the person of the Son, that he descended upon the disciples at Pentecost in flames of fire; that he was the Messiah, the Paraclete, and Jupiter; and that the woman who accompanied him called Helena was Minerva, or the first intelligence."[3]

Because of his exposure to wickedness, Simon, even though he had been born again, needed to walk through a process of inner healing (forgiving, asking for forgiveness, repenting and renouncing his past occult involvement). After that, he could be set free from the demonic influences in his life.

Here are some other possible points of entry that allow a person to become demonized.

Sin. For instance, if you are having sex outside of marriage or have a problem with lust, you need to first stop sinning and repent and then you can be delivered. If this sin was in the past, you need to repent of that before you can be delivered.

Trauma. I have seen people who have been in car accidents become afflicted by a spirit of death, fear or proneness to accidents. Once they have an accident, they have more accidents. Young people who fall in love and are deeply rejected can pick up a spirit of rejection. People who go through a surgical procedure need special prayers of protection from demonic harassment.

Occult involvement. Any of the types of occult involvement I have mentioned in this book can open the door to a demon. At the end of this chapter I have included a special prayer for you to pray to break all demonic attachments from the occult. In the next chapter we will look at generational curses that need to be broken.

Abuse. If you are a victim of sexual, physical or emotional abuse, then you may have a demonic attachment, such as abandonment or rejection. Later in this chapter I will show you how to know if you have need to be delivered of a demonic influence.

Demons Common Among Believers

As someone who travels around the world and visits many churches, it is my observation that many Christians get born again but never go through the process of becoming free from past or present occult influences. As a result, they backslide. If they do not backslide, they often cause tremendous problems in the Church. Harold Caballeros, pastor of El Shaddai Church in Guatemala, says that to bring a person to Christ without taking him through deliverance is like going fishing without cleaning the fish—eventually they will stink![4] Early Church leaders evidently agreed with Caballeros. Since most first-century Christians came out of an occult environment, it was common practice to do exorcisms at the same time as baptisms.[5]

Why did I call this chapter "What! Little Ole Me Have a Demon?" I have witnessed many believers who have demonic influences operating in their lives. Some have a spirit of fear, some a spirit of rejection and others have any of a number of spirits. But each demonized person can be set free. Very few people go through life without some kind of wounding, trauma or other experience that sets them up for a demonic influence of some kind.

Doris Wagner, in her excellent book on deliverance titled *How to Cast Out Demons*, tells about the three-day retreat of Pastor César Castellanos's church in Bogotá, Colombia. Castellanos and his wife, Claudia, had about 50,000 cell groups in their church as of the end of 1998. In this church, every new convert is expected to go on a three-day retreat during which time they are taught the basic Christian doctrines and taken through deliverance and inner healing, which includes the breaking of generational curses. Now that is what I call cleaning the fish![6]

Years ago, Doris and I had dinner with the Castellanoses in Bogotá. Their church had approximately 10,000 members at that time. When we asked them the secret to their church's growth, they replied, "The casting out of demons." People who are freed and healed stay in church. They do not church-hop the way some people do and they are not as easily offended or rejected.

Every church, just like the Castellanoses's in Bogotá, needs a deliverance team and some kind of deliverance ministry to new converts. Sadly, very few churches are equipped in this way. As a result, members who want deliverance ministry must travel to an individual or church that has one. This should not be the situation. Remember, Mark 16:17 declares that it is the pattern for believers to cast out demons. Many Christians have never even cast out one demon! We need to train our church members to fulfill this biblical mandate.

Demonization in the Bible

When we understand how to look for patterns in Scripture, it becomes easy to detect instances in which people in the Bible became demonized. The religious leaders who listened to Stephen were collectively influenced by a religious spirit and a spirit of murder. Note what the Bible says about them: "When they heard these things they were cut to the heart, and they gnashed at him with their teeth. . . . Then they cried out with a loud voice, stopped their ears, and ran at him with one accord" (Acts 7:54, 57).

Saul, the young man who watched these same leaders stone Stephen, was changed and demonized as he watched the murder. The Bible says that after this he made havoc of the Church (see Acts 8:3; 22:4-5, 19-20; 26:9-11). The religious spirit and the spirit of murder on the religious leaders came upon him also.

Gradually Demonized

I have found many times that a person does not become demonized over night. There are usually steps leading up to this. To help fully understand the process, I have compiled a list. Much of the information below comes from Lester Sumrall, who laid out some insightful stages to demonization in his book, *Demons: the Answer Book*.[7] I have combined Sumrall's keen observations with my own, which have been gathered through years of ministry.

> **Regression**. A person in this stage no longer has a desire to read his or her Bible or worship and praise the Lord. Every believer needs to press into God through personal discipleship in study of the Word and worship to break the power of regression.

> **Repression**. The emotions become further repressed. There is not the joy of the Lord expressed through life and voice any longer. This is a lighter bondage that can often be broken by giving the sacrifice of praise in a worship service. One of the first places this can be detected is in the human voice. A person who is repressed has a flat voice without melody.

> **Suppression**. To suppress means to squeeze, crush or press down. A suppressed person feels a general sense of melancholy and lethargy. They do not desire to go to church. My advice to those who are suppressed is to press into God. Tell the devil that he will not win in your life and rebuke him from causing you to have a spirit of heaviness (see Isa. 61:3). You may need to rebuke a spirit

of heaviness in order to be free. Afterward, press into the Lord and ask Him to help you get the joy of the Lord back. A wonderful Scripture for this is, "A merry heart does good, like medicine" (Prov. 17:22).

Depression. People in depression lose their appetites. They often suffer from sleeplessness. In my opinion, depression is not always a spirit, but it can be. I did not believe this until I observed Carlos Annacondia, the Argentine evangelist, have great success with those in a depressed state by casting out the spirit of depression. Since then, I have done the same and seen many set free.

One other note *for women only*: Sometimes we women can be one big hormone. Women may have a problem with depression because of hormonal changes that simply need to be brought into balance. Not everything that happens to us is caused by a demon.

Oppression. Oppressed people have the appearance of being weighed down with problems of the world. They may be very fearful and not able to cope with the burdens of life. They have all the symptoms I have written about here and other symptoms as well.

Obsession. At this stage of demon domination, according to Sumrall, it is doubtful that the person being hurt by Satan could be delivered without the assistance of someone else. The reason for this is that obsession changes the mind. Black becomes white and white seems black. A straight thing is now crooked and a lie becomes the truth. By definition, "obsession" is "a persistent disturbing preoccupation with an often unreasonable idea or feeling."[8]

Demonization.[9] Once people reach full demonization they are controlled in their soul and body by demons. They have given access to their flesh, so the demons rule over their flesh, doing as they will. Their mind is taken over by spirits, so they can no longer control their thought life. When this happens, they need outside help to get free. They can no longer break the power of the demonic influences by themselves.

> WHAT DO DEMONS LIKE TO INHABIT? OF COURSE, THEIR FIRST CHOICE IS HUMAN BEINGS.

This is a rare state for a believer. However, there are cases where this has occurred. Often, at this point, unless they receive deliverance, demonized people will be admitted to a mental institution. It is sad to think that there are born-again believers in mental institutions. I have seen this happen to some who have had deep tragedies in their lives, such as the loss of their whole families, plus a barrage of other terrible circumstances.

WHERE DEMONS LIVE

What do demons like to inhabit? Of course, their first choice is human beings. Examples of this happening are abundant. Many books have been written about this type of oppression and possession, so I will not elaborate on it here.

Demons, however, do not only target humans. If they cannot attack a person directly, they will sometimes settle for an animal. We see that Satan himself chose to inhabit the serpent in order to tempt Eve (see Gen. 3:1). And Jesus sent the "unclean spirits" into the swine (see Mark 5:13).

Satan will use whatever means he can to demonize whomever or whatever he can. When I first went to Argentina, my family found out quite a bit about this. In Argentina, we saw great breakthrough in ministry. Since the demons were not successful with a direct attack on anyone in my family, they came at us in another way.

When in Doubt, Cast it Out

One day, while we were living in Weatherford, Texas, and I had just begun my travels to Argentina, I heard our nice little black kitty let out a yelp from the back porch. When I went out to check on him, he snarled, scratched and yowled like a banshee from hell. I definitely knew something other than our sweet pet was in that cat.

When our cat began to yelp, I called Mike, who was at a meeting: "Mike, will you come home as soon as you can? Our cat has a demon." At that time Mike did *not* believe that an animal could be demonized. Mike came home after a while and looked at me like I had lost my mind! Being the brilliant, analytical, Mr. Computer Brain sort in those days, he said, "Oh, Cindy, our cat doesn't have a demon."

"OK," I answered, "then you go find out what's wrong with him."

Mike reached down to pet that sweet kitty. No sooner did he reach out his hand than that cat let out the same demonic yowl I had heard before. Our cat then growled and ran off under the car! Mike turned back to me and gasped, "Cindy, the cat does have a demon!" I knew that it was not politically correct to enjoy the moment too much, so I murmured, "Perhaps we should take authority over it and set it free," which we did. By the next morning, we had our affectionate little pet back.

Never Too Young

It is hard not to get into some intense storytelling—there have been so many experiences! But I will restrain myself and limit it to one more.

When I was traveling regularly back and forth to Argentina, it was fairly common for our pets to be demonized. One day when our son Daniel was eight years old, he ran in with a snarling cat he was holding by the scruff of its neck. He threw him under the dining-room table and yelled to me in the other room, "Mom, that thing is back again!"

"Daniel," I replied, "you cast it out!"

"Mom," he answered, "I'm trying to play. You come deal with it."

The point is that he knew how to deliver the cat from the demon and he was not afraid, but he simply was too busy playing to want to mess with it.

Does Not Need to Be Alive

Objects as well as animals can have demonic attachments. The city of Jericho was accursed by God and the people of Israel were not to take anything from the city except for the silver and gold and precious metals that the Lord said were to go into the treasury of the house of the Lord (see Josh. 6:18-19). The city was burned with fire, for this was the way in which accursed objects were to be dealt (see Josh. 10:15).

Later, after the Israelites lost at Ai (see Josh. 7), the Lord told Joshua that they had been defeated because there were accursed things in their camp. It was discovered that Achan had buried objects from Jericho in his tent. He, his whole family and all of their possessions were destroyed with fire and the curse was broken. Note that the curse affected not only him but also his family and the entire tribe.

I have included an appendix on ridding your home of objects that may have demonic attachments.

If you have acquired antique furniture and have never prayed over it, I strongly recommend that you do so. That wonderful Victorian chiffonier or eighteenth-century oak settle can come with "hitchhikers" from previous owners. My daughter once was having terrible nightmares. They completely stopped after we prayed over her antique headboard.

DELIVERANCE

How do we know if we need deliverance?

It is important to discern whether the problem is simply your flesh running rampant or a demonic influence. Instead of mortifying the flesh and casting out demons, some people mistakenly want to crucify demons and cast out the flesh. Not everything is a demon, yet we do not want to discount that it might be one. I have heard deliverance ministers say, "When in doubt, cast it out." Sometimes the problem will have been caused by the flesh and not a demon at all. But even if there was a demon involved, you may need to break the habit patterns you developed or stop doing whatever it was that allowed the demon to be present in your life. For example, if the demon came into your life because you were regularly having your fortune told by a soothsayer, it is not enough to simply get deliverance. You must also stop seeing the fortune-teller! You need to find out the roots of why you are doing what you are doing, or the spirit could come back seven times worse (see Matt. 12:45).

A person needs deliverance if the following either has occurred or is happening now:

1. recurring problems—addictions that you are driven to participate in rather than something you can stop at any moment;
2. occult involvement;
3. molestation (if you have been molested or if you have been a perpetrator);
4. an adopted child (often adopted children deal with the spirit of rejection or the spirit of abandonment);
5. inordinate fear of dying, frequent driving thoughts of death or a death wish;
6. extreme religious legalism;
7. overwhelming desire to control or manipulate;
8. membership in a secret society such as the Freemasons.

You may also need deliverance from a family spirit that has demonized your bloodline from generation to generation (see chapter 10). Sometimes there may be a familiar, or familial spirit. I will discuss this more fully in the next chapter on breaking curses.

If you ever asked for a spirit guide while you were involved in New Age practices, you will need to dismiss it. Also, if your children tell you that they have an imaginary friend, do not take this lightly (see chapter 3). It is possible that it is a spirit guide trying to attach itself to your child—not just the child being cute.

It is important for you to read this chapter and the next one in their entireties to receive the knowledge you need in order to be free from the power of occult involvement that may be in your life. There are also a number of excellent books on deliverance (see recommended reading at the back of this book).

When to Receive

You may or may not know that you need deliverance. Here are some ways that may determine if you do:

1. Discerning of spirits: This is the supernatural gift.
2. Fruit of the spirit: I mentioned this earlier. When you are driven or out of control in a certain area of your life, the kind of fruit you bear will tell you who or what is driving you. And if that area of your life is truly out of control, that spirit influencing you is surely demonic.
3. Occult involvement: If you have been involved with the occult for any length of time, you most likely have some kind of demonic attachment that you must remove.

How to Receive

If you have determined that you need deliverance, then please follow through on it. If you know of a credible deliverance ministry, make an appointment and go for help. If you do not know anyone you can trust, it is possible that you can pray for yourself. Some people receive quite a bit of deliverance through "truth encounter" ministries such as those mentioned in Neil Anderson's books.[10]

Likewise, some people receive quite a bit of deliverance when they are born again or have a deep experience with the Holy Spirit. It is not clear why this happens with some people and not with others.

As you say the prayer at the end of this chapter, realize that you have absolute authority through the name of Jesus Christ to cast out demons. Here are three Scriptures to encourage you:

Therefore submit to God. Resist the devil and he will flee from you (James 4:7).

Behold, I give you the authority to trample on serpents and scorpions, and over all the power of the enemy, and nothing shall by any means hurt you (Luke 10:19).

But if I cast out demons with the finger of God, surely the kingdom of God has come upon you (Luke 11:20).

Steps to Freedom

Regardless of whether you are going to go for ministry with a deliverance minister, you will need to go through the following steps: forgiveness, repentance and renunciation.

Forgiveness: Make a list of those people whom you need to forgive and forgive them.

Repentance: Repent for any known sin, past or present, in your life.

Renunciation: Renounce any occult involvement or influence in your life.

Have you been marking that list on page 203? Now is the time to review it. Add any areas of occult involvement in your life that you have not already included. Then use the list as you say the following prayer:

> *Father God, I now repent for all occult involvement, forgive me for participating in those practices that are forbidden by You in Your Word. I now renounce and repent from my involvement in:* (insert the items you have checked on your list).

After you have gone through the process of renunciation, pray this prayer to bind any demonic powers that may have in any way demonized you:

> *Father, in the name of Jesus Christ of Nazareth, I now bind and take authority over all demonic spirits, which may have*

attached themselves to me. Demonic spirit, I forbid you from
manifesting or harming me or my family in any way. I cover
myself with the Blood of Jesus Christ and ask You, Father God,
to send Your angels to protect me, my family, my loved ones
and my possessions. In Jesus' name. Amen.

You can pray for deliverance at the end of the next chapter. It is important to deal with the iniquities of the generations before you pray the deliverance prayer, so you can be truly free.

Notes

1. Gordon Lindsay, *The Origin of Demons and Their Orders* (Dallas, TX: Christ for the Nations Publishing), p. 8.
2. Derek Prince, *They Shall Expel Demons* (Grand Rapids, MI: Chosen Books, 1998), p. 89.
3. Finis Jennings Dake, *The Dake Annotated Reference Bible* (Lawrenceville, GA: Dake Publishing, 1963), p. 131.
4. I have heard Harold Caballeros say this from the pulpit many times.
5. Kilian McDonnell and George T. Montague, *Christian Initiation and Baptism in the Holy Spirit: Evidence from the First Eight Centuries* (Collegeville, MN: The Liturgical Press, 1994), p. 8-9.
6. Doris Wagner, *How to Cast Out Demons* (Ventura, CA: Renew Books, 2000), pp. 42–44.
7. Lester Sumrall, *Demons: the Answer Book* (South Bend, IN: Whitaker House, 1993), pp. 80-96.
8. *Merriam-Webster's Collegiate Dictionary,* 10th ed., s.v. "obsession."
9. This is where I differ from Sumrall's list. He calls the next step posession, while I call it demonization.
10. Neil T. Anderson, *Victory over the Darkness* (Ventura, CA: Regal Books, 1990).

CHECKLIST

Renounce any of the following practices that you have been
involved in at any level at any time in your life, from simple dabbling to full participation. Remember that reading your horoscope, playing with a Ouija board or wondering who you were in
a past life is dabbling and needs to be renounced. Use this list
when you say the prayer on page 201.

___ Astral projection
___ Astrology
___ Black Magic
___ Church of Satan
___ Crystal healing
___ Crystal-ball reading
___ Divination
___ Dungeons and Dragons (and
    other occult games)
___ E.S.P.
___ Goddess worship
___ I Ching
___ Idolatry
___ Kabbalah
___ Macumba
___ Membership or participation in
    secret societies (such as freema-
    sonry and Eastern Star)
___ Mind control
___ New Age practices
___ Other occult religions
___ Ouija board
___ Palm reading
___ Palo Mayombe
___ Powwow magic

___ Psychic healing
___ Rainbow Gathering
___ Reincarnation
___ Rune-stone casting
___ Santeria
___ Satanism
___ Soothsaying
___ Spirits, spiritualism
___ Tantra
___ Tarot-card reading
___ Tea-leaf reading
___ Temple of Set
___ Umbanda
___ Vampirism
___ Voodoo
___ Water witching, or
    dowsing
___ Wicca
___ Anything else involving the
    occult

Other Activities

___
___
___
___

CHAPTER 10

BREAKING CURSES

A number of years ago I received a frantic call from a member of our church. The voice on the other end of the line sounded panicky and frightened. As I listened, the person shared how her daughter had recently had surgery and come through just fine. However, for seemingly no apparent reason, the daughter went into a rapid decline and was placed in Intensive Care. The doctors were totally perplexed.

The mother said to me, "Cindy, can you come? None of the doctors know what to do. She is thrashing around and has to be restrained, and her condition is deteriorating."

As the mother talked, I took in what she said, while carefully tuning into the voice of the Lord as well. The Holy Spirit spoke to me during the conversation and said, "She has a death curse. Go to the hospital and break it." For the moment, feeling that it was wiser to keep this information to myself, I told the mother that I would be glad to go and pray for her daughter.

As I drove to the hospital, I knew that it might be challenging to get in to see her in the Intensive Care Unit. Pondering what to do, I felt the Lord said the direct approach was best. I simply walked into ICU, told them that I was her minister and that I had to see her immediately. To my surprise, they let me see her right away.

BREAKING THE DEATH CURSE

When I entered the room, I was shocked at my friend's appearance. She was strapped down, thrashing wildly and seemed to be in some kind of altered state. I opened my Bible to Psalm 91 and read the passage aloud to her. I bent down and whispered, "Susan, (not her real name) you have been cursed with a death curse and you are afraid you are going to die. You are not going to die. I am going to break the curse right now, and you are going to be just fine."

Then, in the same quiet tone of voice, I said, "In the Name of Jesus Christ, I break your curse of death. You spirit of death, you will let go of your hold on Susan's life and leave her this minute." After the prayer, Susan quieted and seemed to be resting. I stood over her a few moments and prayed a healing prayer and then left.

The next morning I had a call from a very joyful mother who said, "Cindy, thanks for praying! Her recovery has been nothing short of remarkable. She woke up this morning and was so much better that she is back in her own room, sitting up talking and eating, and the doctors still do not know what was wrong with her."

At this point I shared with her that I had broken a death curse over Susan's life and had prayed for her healing. Her mother was amazed and hung up thanking me and thanking, most of all, the Lord Jesus Christ.

I am aware that this story may sound very strange to some people. A death curse? Surely things like this do not really happen in this day and age!

A Death Curse

Let me tell yet another story. Several years ago I was ministering at an evangelical church in the eastern part of the United States. Keep in mind that this was not a charismatic congregation. As I ministered, I suddenly had a word of knowledge that there were people in the congregation whose family members had died from being cursed to death.

This all seemed rather odd, even to me. However, I knew it was the Holy Spirit's prompting to ask if anyone had family members who had died that way. To my surprise, around 10 people came forward. I began to interview them, and one by one they told me of the terrible deaths that various family members had suffered after being cursed. One died by drowning, and others had similar improbable deaths.

This introduced me to powwow magic, which I covered in chapter 4. Prevalent in some churches in Pennsylvania, it is a mixture of witchcraft and Christian beliefs. I asked those in the congregation to repent for their families who had practiced this kind of witchcraft. The pastor's own mother had been a practicing witch—he prayed for those whose families had been cursed to death.

I also asked those who felt they had received a death curse to stand. It was startling how many rose to receive prayer. Some of the people wept. They also forgave those who had done this evil against them. That was a very eye-opening experience for me!

People who are cursed live defeated lives. They are constantly getting sick, experiencing poverty and becoming depressed. Usually, not only are they defeated, but their parents were also defeated.

HAVE YOU BEEN CURSED?

This chapter will not only help you understand what curses are, but it will also help you know if you have been cursed. There are many different kinds of curses but, if you are a Christian, they do not have to prosper against you.

When discussing the subject of breaking curses, it is critical to understand that God Himself thought this subject was so important that He had Moses command the children of Israel to stand on two mountains when they crossed over into the Promised Land. The Lord had the Levites speak in a loud voice to His people. They spoke out both the curses for disobedience and the blessings that come for obedience. While many Christians have studied the blessings, not as many of us are aware of what actually causes a curse to come if we are disobedient.

> THERE ARE MANY DIFFERENT KINDS OF CURSES BUT, IF YOU ARE A CHRISTIAN, THEY DO NOT HAVE TO PROSPER AGAINST YOU.

The curses as given in Deuteronomy 27:15-26 includes the following things:

1. making of carved or molded image for the purpose of idolatry, which is strictly forbidden (see Exod. 20:3-5);
2. treating your father or mother with contempt (see Exod. 20:12);
3. making the blind wander off the road;
4. perverting the justice due to the stranger, the fatherless and the widow;
5. sexual sins of various kinds, such as incest, sodomy and adultery;
6. secretly attacking your neighbor;
7. taking a bribe to murder;
8. not observing all the words of this Law.

However, the cursing does not end here. Deuteronomy 28:15-68 goes into much more depth. Christian teacher Derek Prince, in his book *Blessing or Curse,* gives this list of curses drawn from Deuteronomy:

1. humiliation;
2. barrenness, unfruitfulness;
3. mental and physical sickness;
4. family breakdown;
5. poverty;
6. defeat;
7. oppression;
8. failure;
9. God's disfavor.[1]

The Head and the Tail

Of course, God also gave the children of Israel a list of blessings they would receive if they obeyed Him. Prince also said this about the blessings:

> I once asked the Lord to show me how this would apply in my life. I felt He gave me this answer: The head makes the decisions and the tail just gets dragged around.[2]

Some of you reading this chapter may feel more like the tail than the head—like you are getting dragged around in life. It is possible that you have been cursed; particularly if you or someone in your family has had some kind of occult involvement. I am writing this as the final chapter, so you can close the last pages of this book set free and walking in victory in all that Jesus bought for you on the cross.

I have always found that God is very smart. He has written things in the Bible and placed them in such a way for us to understand their importance in our lives. In other words, the instructions He gave to the children of Israel were to be followed precisely in the order He gave them. As children of God, we have been grafted onto the vine, and thus, are also inheritors of the blessings of Abraham today (see Gal. 3:13-14).

What am I saying? In order for the children of Israel to take the Promised Land, they had to understand what brought the blessings and what brought the curses. I am saying that we also need this today. There are many people walking around who are cursed in various ways who know they are defeated but do not know what to do about it. This chapter will start you down the path to freedom from those curses.

Spotting a Curse

There are indicators that you have been cursed. Of course, some of these can stem from other sources as well. Many times a pattern or combination of factors means you are suffering from a curse of some kind. Throughout many years of helping people become free of curses, I have learned to recognize some indicators:

1. sudden, unexplainable illness (by this I mean the doctor simply cannot find any natural, known cause);
2. sudden dizziness or fainting spells;
3. severe headaches;
4. sharp, unexplained pains (a voodoo curse can cause this);
5. insanity in your family line;
6. a pattern of infirmities in a person or family;
7. poverty;
8. barrenness;
9. disfavor.

When dealing with the subject of curses, we not only pray for a person, but we also ask them to get a physical checkup, especially if they are having patterns of infirmity, such as headaches or dizziness. One way to know if you have broken a curse is when the symptoms do not return.

Source of Curses

We need to understand that a curse cannot prosper against us for very long without there being some open door in our lives. Proverbs 26:2 declares: "Like a flitting sparrow, like a flying swallow, so a curse without cause shall not alight."

A curse can come from something you have done, be a result of family iniquity that produces generational curses or be an outside attack from someone involved in the occult. It is also possible for a person to suffer from a curse when someone in the Body of Christ says false prayers.

Opening the Door

There are numbers of ways that we can open the door to allow a curse to prosper against us. Here are a few of them:

1. unforgiveness;
2. occult involvement;
3. idolatry;
4. ownership of objects forbidden in the Bible;
5. failure to tithe;
6. oaths taken during secret society ceremonies such as those in freemasonry, Eastern Star and similar groups;
7. generational iniquities.

I could write a book on the subject of breaking curses, just as each of the points I just mentioned could easily be a chapter in and of itself. Instead, to help you gain a deeper understanding, I will give you some excellent reference material to read on this and other subjects covered in this book.

Generational Ties

The biggest open door to curses are generational iniquities. Generational iniquities are an open door to generational curses that have been passed down through the family bloodline. The Bible refers to these in a number of places, including Exodus 20:5:

> You shall not bow down to them nor serve them. For I, the LORD your God, am a jealous God, visiting the iniquity of the fathers on the children to the third and fourth generations of those who hate Me.

Many people are confused about iniquities, because they do not know there is a difference between sin and iniquity. The Bible speaks of them a number of times as two different things (see Ps. 32:5, "the iniquity of my sin"). Sin is basically the cause, and iniquity includes the effect. Generational iniquity works like this: A parent can commit a sin such as occult involvement or sexual sin—that produces a curse. The curse then causes a generational iniquity, or weakness, to pass down in the family line.

Here is an illustration: A pregnant woman has an X ray and as a result of the radiation the unborn child becomes deformed. The fetus, who did not order the X ray, nonetheless, is affected by it and becomes a victim. Sin, like the X ray, damages the generations to come. This is an awesome thought and should put the fear of the Lord in us before we enter into sin.[3]

To summarize: When we sin, if the sin is not repented of, any children that we have after this sin will reap what we have sown through what the Bible calls iniquity. This iniquity can come in the form of a spiritual bondage, such as different forms of addiction, or as a driving weakness for sexual sin or perversion. It might be that all your children will be extremely accident prone or live a life of extreme poverty.

The good news is that Jesus paid the price not only for our sin but also for the iniquities of our forefathers! Iniquities will not affect our eternal salvation, but they do affect the quality of life we have on this earth. Isaiah 53:1-13 explains that He (Jesus) bore not only our sins, but our iniquities. He became a curse for us, so that we can be free!

Christ has redeemed us from the curse of the law, having become a curse for us. For it is written, "Cursed is everyone who hangs on a tree" (Gal. 3:13).

THREE PRIMARY CURSES

There are three main curses that come as a result of breaking God's law. They can be found in Deuteronomy 28:15-68. These are the curses of poverty, infirmity and insanity.

The Curse of Poverty

A nation whom you have not known shall eat the fruit of your land and the produce of your labor, and you shall be only oppressed and crushed continually. . . . You shall carry much seed out to the field and gather but little in, for the locust shall consume it (Deut. 28:33,38).

How do we know that we have a curse of poverty? We just got our car fixed, and our washing machine breaks. We fix our washing machine and our plumbing springs a leak. We usually have a large credit-card debt with such high interest rates that we are only able to pay the interest, and we get further and further into a hole.

One open door to a curse of poverty is robbing God. If your parents or their parents were not tithers, this means they were God robbers (see Mal. 3:8-9). This Scripture declares that you are cursed if you do not tithe. I have found that people who tithe and do not receive a blessing are often suffering because their parents or grandparents did not tithe.

Another major open door to the curse of poverty, of course, is idolatry. If you or any member of your family worshiped idols, were given a saint's name or participated in any kind of occult practices, a curse is produced.

> THE GOOD NEWS IS THAT JESUS PAID THE PRICE NOT ONLY FOR OUR SIN BUT ALSO FOR THE INIQUITIES OF OUR FOREFATHERS!

I once ministered to a lady in southern Argentina whose family had a curse that caused the firstborn son in every generation to die early. They had a curse of early death. She repented of her family's idolatry, and we broke this dreadful curse.

Named After a Saint

It is common in some families to name a son or daughter after a saint. This may be done out of tradition or respect. But if, through the years, the family or Church has worshiped the particular saint as an idol, demons may have attached themselves to the name. If you were given a saint's name, you should renounce all such attachments. Remember that you are denouncing the demons and the idolization of that saint, not the saint himself or herself.

You do not have to change your name unless you feel a leading from the Holy Spirit to do so. Sometimes the worship of a particular saint in a family line is so strong that a person needs to make a clean break and change his or her name; at other times simply renouncing the allegiance is enough.

Demonic links to certain names do not occur only in the western Church. Many believers in Asia take a Christian name upon conversion because their given name was tied to the occult or had been given to them through divination.

It is exciting to see the fruit of the freedom and change that comes in a believer's life after that person is free from the curse of poverty. Pastors all across Latin America have told me that they were able to buy a car or a house for the first time in their life and provide for their family after being set free from this terrible curse.

We will break any curses that you have upon your life at the end of this chapter. You might want to make a list as you read and keep a journal on what you think the open door might have been that allowed the curse, so you can repent later.

The Curse of Infirmity

> The LORD will strike you with consumption, with fever, with inflammation, with severe burning fever, with the sword, with scorching, and with mildew; they shall pursue you until you perish. . . . The LORD will strike you with the boils of Egypt, with tumors, with the scab, and with the itch, from which you cannot be healed (Deut. 28:22,27).

How do we know if we have a curse of infirmity? We just get over the flu, and we break our toe. Our toe gets better, and we get a blood disease. If it is a family curse, the same pattern will happen with our children. Of course, this all ties into poverty as well, because a cursed person would usually have high medical bills.

The Curse of Insanity

> The LORD will strike you with madness and blindness and confusion of heart (Deut. 28:28).

Often insanity runs in the family line. Different kinds of mental conditions such as manic depression also show up in generation after generation. I have found that the propensity to premenstrual syndrome (PMS) and difficult female cycles can also be related to a curse of idolatry in the bloodline.

Breaking the Power

The first person who tries to break the pattern of iniquity and curses in a family line may have quite a struggle. Both the demonic spirits and physical patterns or weaknesses have been established in some for many generations.

There is sometimes quite a battle to break their power even after the curse is broken. Please do not become discouraged if you are in a great battle. You are fighting not only for yourself but also for generations to come. You may be the only believer in your whole family line and are standing in the gap for them. Ask others in your spiritual family to pray with you until your whole family is set free. Of course, as I noted earlier, you may need counseling (as well as inner healing, which is basically forgiveness) to walk in total freedom. You need to understand the patterns to break, so you will not fall into the same kinds of sins again. An excellent book to read on this subject is *Deliverance and Inner Healing* by John and Mark Sandford.

In addition to generation curses, it is possible that you may have been cursed from someone in the occult, as I mentioned in the example of powwow magic. I have also mentioned the curses Satanists will put upon those they consider unworthy or simply a nuisance.

No Weapon Shall Prevail
Christians need to understand that just as there is heaven's intercession, there is also hell's intercession. I first learned about

this from my friend Margaret Moberly. Some occultists will hate people to death through spells and chanting. Others will sacrifice and release demons to go after Christians to bring death and poverty. The good news is that none of these curses has a right to prosper against you.

> No weapon formed against you shall prosper, and every tongue which rises against you in judgment you shall condemn. This is the heritage of the servants of the LORD (Isa. 54:17).

Note that this Scripture does not say that the weapon will not be formed or sent, but that it will not prosper. We need to stay pure and holy before the Lord, walking in forgiveness, so that we will not have any holes in our armor for the evil one to attack. Jesus said, "for the ruler [some translations such as *KJV* say "prince"] of this world is coming and he has nothing in Me" (John 14:30).

A curse may try to strike us, but it cannot prosper if we are walking in a right place with God.

Here are some possible open doors through which an occult curse can strike you:

1. strife;
2. unforgiveness;
3. trauma;
4. failure to tithe;
5. forsaking assembly together with believers (we are commanded not to do so);
6. witchcraft in the church;
7. anti-Semitism.

Sudden Attacks

An occult curse strikes suddenly. This is why we need to listen to the Holy Spirit each day, since He will warn us of impending attacks. Praise God, if we are not spiritually sensitive enough, God will often warn our friends and intercessors to pray for us.

One day I was reading a book to my daughter, Mary, when I suddenly became extremely dizzy and faint. It hit with a viciousness that I knew was supernatural. I quietly said to Mary, "Honey, why don't you go play in your room for a little while?" I then called my friend, Margaret Moberly. She prayed with me and broke the curse. After that I was completely fine and the dizziness did not return. Another time I was walking through my house and, in one moment, the left side of my body went numb all the way from my head to my feet! I again called Margaret and she said that I had been hit with a curse known as "stun and numb." She broke the curse and all the symptoms immediately left.

Accidents Happen

Occult curses can cause accidents. A fall down the stairs where you feel like you were pushed, a fire that starts mysteriously or other bizarre occurrences may be the end result of a curse. If the curse is done through a blood sacrifice, it will be stronger. Sometimes those in the occult will sacrifice a finger or a body part. At other times, they offer some other kind of sacrifice to strengthen the power of demons they send against you. Sometimes certain intersections of the city will be cursed and repeatedly accidents will take place. They need to be prayed for and the curse of accidents lifted.

At times, when a curse sent against a certain person cannot prosper, it will rebound against the sender or will affect something close to the intended victim, either in affections or proximity. I have known several instances of this. Years ago, the house across the street from Peter Wagner burned down during one of our first Spiritual Warfare Network meetings. The intercessors felt that a curse had been sent against him as we had prayed against any destruction that would come against him.

Another time, I had prayed against a spirit of death sent against a friend of mine. She was fine, but a friend of hers dropped dead in her kitchen that week. Therefore, I have learned to be sensitive to the Holy Spirit's leading to totally break the effect of the curse from prospering at all, against anyone.

Some family lines have a death curse on them, and the descendants die at an early age. This was the case in my father's family, and we have prayed to break that off of our generation. My father died early, as did his father before him, as well as most of his brothers and sisters and his mother.

Curses Against Locations

Land can be cursed as well as people, and the curses will affect those who live there. I wrote about this in the chapter on demonology. *Releasing Heaven to Earth* by Alistair Petrie is an excellent book on breaking curses off the land. Alistair is an Anglican leader from Canada and has seen remarkable results in what could be termed "healing the land" (2 Chron. 7:14).

We find a powerful example of healing the land in Joshua 6:26 where Joshua pronounced, "Cursed be the man before the LORD who rises up and builds this city Jericho; he shall lay its foundation with his firstborn, and with his youngest he shall set up its gates."

This indeed came to pass when Hiel of Bethel built Jericho. One Kings 16:34 reveals that Hiel laid Jericho's foundation "with Abiram his firstborn, and with his youngest son Segub he set up its gates, according to the word of the LORD, which He had spoken through Joshua the son of Nun."

Protecting Your Loved Ones

Another possible attack from cursing can come against us or our loved ones during a surgical procedure. It is important to pray over loved ones while they are in the hospital, since occultists will sometimes take advantage of them while they are either under anesthetic or helpless in some other way. Be sensitive to your friend or relative after surgery to see if he or she is acting strangely or not recovering as anticipated.

I do not want to create a scare, making people nervous about going into hospitals. There are many excellent doctors and nurses. I do not want anyone to be paranoid about getting medical help; we just need to be spiritually sensitive.

Another open door to a death curse is trauma and rejection. One time before I went to Argentina, I received a call from someone very close to me. This person was upset at me for teaching on spiritual warfare and told me so. She went on to claim that many people close to me were supposedly having problems as a result of my teaching.

I did not realize how this had affected me until I got home from the trip. During the trip I had led a group in prayer against San la Muerte, or the Spirit of Death. After church one day, I laid down and, all of a sudden, I knew I was dying. I could literally feel the life leaving my body. I quickly called my husband, Mike, and pleaded with him to call the intercessors. "Mike, I'm dying," I said. Since I had never before said anything like that to Mike, he took it seriously and quickly phoned our prayer partners.

Later, after the curse had been broken, I asked the Lord what the open door for that curse had been. He said, "Cindy, you remember that phone call? You have unforgiveness in your heart toward that person and you have been hurt by them." Needless to say, I quickly and completely forgave! In fact, I was very motivated to do so!

Secret Societies

A major door that many people have in their lives comes from a generational curse that goes back to their families' involvement in secret societies, particularly freemasonry. I recommend that anyone whose ancestors have been involved in these groups do an in-depth study. There are some excellent books written on the subject such as Ron Campbell's *Free from Freemasonry*. There are actually curses that are released against the family during the taking of the vows by those entering the various levels of freemasonry.[4]

One source of curses that is often overlooked comes from within the Church itself—witchcraft in the Church. The Bible says that one of the works of the flesh is witchcraft or sorcery (see Gal. 5:20). How does this operate? One way in which witchcraft functions is through manipulation, control, intimidation and rebellion (see 1 Sam. 15:23).

False Prayers

Some Christians try to control and manipulate other Christians through what I call false prayers. They pray their own will rather than the will of the Father, unaware they have crossed the line into witchcraft. Our words are so powerful! Proverbs 18:21 declares "death and life are in the power of the tongue, and those who love it will eat its fruit."

I have seen pastors and leaders become terribly confused over word curses because of false prayers and even strong statements made by other believers. This is why it is important not to pray amiss but to learn to pray Scripture. When we do this, we release our leaders and friends to the will of God, rather than our own will. I covered this in the chapter titled "Flaky Intercession" in my first book, *Possessing the Gates of the Enemy*. Rick Godwin also has a good book out on this subject. It is titled *Exposing Witchcraft in the Church*.

How do we know if we have had a word curse put on us by another believer? We may suddenly feel confused and unable to clearly hear the voice of the Lord. When this happens, we might, in the name of Jesus Christ, take authority over any word curse or false word sent to manipulate us.

Anti-Semitism

One last, but not least, open door to cursing is that of anti-Semitism. God promised to the children of Abraham in Genesis 12:3: "I will curse him who curses you."

If we have any kind of prejudice against Jewish people, which is anti-Semitism, in our bloodline, it can bring a curse upon our finances and life. In fact, one of the keys to the healing of the economy in Argentina was for Argentinians to repent for having harbored German war criminals and boatloads of Nazi gold!

How to Get Free from a Curse

Now, at last, we get to the good part: the cleansing and getting free from any effects of cursing in your life! I am excited to have reached this point and am very blessed to get to be a part of your release into total freedom in Christ.

Prayer for Salvation

Of course, the first step to getting free is to make sure that you are a born-again believer. If you are not sure that you would go to heaven if you died today, then we need to stop and pray together, so you can know that for certain that you are a blood-bought child of the living God. It is only through the name of Jesus Christ that you can be free from the curses operating in your life.

Let's take a moment and pray together. (If you have been heavily involved in the occult, I suggest you pray this prayer with someone else and that you first renounce all involvement with spirit guides.)

> *Dear God, I ask You to forgive my sins. I repent for every way*
> *I have not obeyed Your word. Please forgive me. Lord Jesus,*
> *will You now come in and take complete control of my life? Be*
> *the Lord of my life from this moment on. I want to be Your*
> *child. Thank You, Lord, for setting me free. Thank You for*
> *allowing me to be Your child from this day on. In the Name of*
> *Jesus Christ. Amen.*

After you have prayed this prayer, you never need doubt again whether or not you are a Christian. God willing, you will not die tonight. Yet whenever you do pass from this life, now that you have said this prayer, you will go straight to heaven to live with the Lord Jesus Christ.

Take Stock of Your Life
The next step to take after making sure that you are right with God is to take stock of your life. Take time to ask the Holy Spirit to show you if you have any unforgiveness in your life. Make a list of anyone you need to forgive, both those still living and those who have already passed away. Then specifically pray and release each person. Here is a sample prayer to help you:

> *Dear God, I now forgive _____. I forgive*
> *them for (whatever way they hurt you or your family or oth-*
> *ers). I now release them to You and ask You to heal any hurt in*
> *my heart associated with (whatever the situation was*
> *that caused you pain).*

In addition, make a list of any family sins that may have been committed. These should include spiritual bondages such as sexual sin. Something I have not yet mentioned is the curse of illegitimacy that even goes down to the tenth generation.

One of illegitimate birth shall not enter the congregation of the LORD; even to the tenth generation none of
his descendants shall enter the congregation of the
LORD (Deut. 23:2).

How does this curse work? If you have a curse of illegitimacy, you will never feel like you have a place in the Church no matter how hard you try—you always feel like you are on the outside
looking in. I have broken this curse off many people. It is amazing the difference they feel after they have repented for illegitimacy in their family line and the curse is broken!

By now you should have repented for any occult involvement in your life. If you have not done so, please go back and
read the section on demonology in chapter 9.

In addition, if you or any member of your family has been
involved in any kind of idolatry, please stop and repent right
now. Later in this section, after I explain how they operate in
one's life, we will have prayer with you to break the power of the
iniquities you may have inherited. Idolatry includes praying to
anyone other than Jesus Christ and bowing down to false gods,
as well as sacrificing to them.

A sample prayer for forgiveness for idolatry might sound like
this:

> *Father God, I now repent for the sins of my fathers to the third
> and fourth and even to the tenth generations. Please forgive all
> forms of idolatrous worship such as* (name the ways your
> family worshiped idols). *Please forgive me for this sin and
> release my family from the curses associated with idolatry.*

DESTROYING OCCULT OBJECTS

There are certain occult objects that we are not to possess. If we own any of the following objects, we need to get rid of them. If the object was at any time worshiped as a god or used in the worship of a false god, then we should burn it or otherwise destroy it.

It is not unusual for tourists to bring home keepsakes from faraway lands that have demonic attachments or are idols. What we often do not realize is that these objects can curse us. For instance, many people purchase African masks that have been used in worship ceremonies. Others buy native art such as Kachina dolls, statues of Hindu gods and statues of Buddha. Back home, havoc starts to reign in the form of sickness, tragedy, depression or marriage break-ups—usually the person does not know why these things have happened. Other people bring home seemingly innocent items, but, as I wrote in the last chapter, they can have spiritual attachments and may need to be discarded or destroyed.

Book Burning in Argentina

Years ago, when Doris Wagner and I were in Resistencia, Argentina, the Lord gave her the idea that we should have people bring their occult objects, light a fire and burn them, following the example recorded in Acts 19:19. Scripture says that after the objects were burned in Ephesus, the Word of the Lord grew mightily and prevailed.

The leaders of the meetings in Argentina decided to burn the objects in a big oil drum. Doris instructed the people to wrap the objects with newspaper if the people did not want others to know what they were bringing. At the beginning of the meeting, in response to a prior announcement, people brought a wide assortment of occult objects. Some people also carried objects that had caused them to be in some kind of bondage or another. People brought idols, love potions, Macumba paraphernalia, pornographic magazines and unknown objects wrapped in newspaper.

The leaders poured gasoline into the oil drum and then lit it with fire. What happened next was startling! As the occult objects burned, some of the people actually screamed and cried out in anguish as demons manifested themselves. Many people came forward seeking deliverance from these occult spirits. Then, just as happened in Ephesus centuries ago, many people came forward and were saved.

I think Church leaders today should consider having similar book burnings. Pastor Jim Marocco did this when he planted a church on the island of Maui. He had people bring and burn occult items, specifically objects that were worshiped as part of their native religions. After the objects were destroyed, his church experienced great growth.

Inspect Your House

Before we finish praying in this chapter, go around your house and ask the Lord what you need to get rid of. Some objects you may just need to pray over. Remember, you cannot get rid of those things that are not yours. However, you can bind the spirits attached to them and forbid them from manifesting in your house. For an excellent, more in-depth study of spiritual house cleansing, I suggest that you read *Ridding Your Home of Spiritual Darkness* by Chuck Pierce and Rebecca Wagner Sytsema.

Prayer to Break Generational Curses

Now, at last, you are ready to pray and break the power of the curses that you might have inherited or that have in some way been sent against you from outside sources. It would be wonderful to pray this with your whole family, if this is possible. You can pray the prayers alone, but it is great to have a friend or prayer partner pray with you to stand in the gap as you renounce the curses and get free.

Remember, through the name of Jesus Christ and His shed blood, you have absolute authority to break these curses. Also, you do not have to be afraid. Luke 10:19 promises:

> Behold, I give you the authority to trample on serpents and scorpions, and over all the power of the enemy, and nothing shall by any means hurt you.

Do you have your list ready? All right, let's begin! We will first deal with any generational iniquities or curses that you have not previously repented for and broken. Pray this prayer with me out loud, if you can:

> *Father, in the Name of Jesus Christ of Nazareth, I now appropriate the power of the blood of the Lamb and claim that nothing by any means shall harm me as I pray this prayer, nor will anything cause harm to my family or any of our possessions.*

> *Father, I now repent for the generational sin committed by my family to the third, fourth, and even tenth generations for the following things: (name each one).*

Before reading your list, it is important that you realize that you are not praying for the dead in this prayer, nor can you repent on behalf of anyone else, dead or alive. This prayer is not on behalf of their sin, but because they sinned. It closes the open door Satan has been using to come against you and your family. It gives you the legal right to have the curses broken off your life and the lives of others in your family.

Now read your list. It might include some of the following:

- Idolatry. This includes the breaking of ties with all saints' names that have been worshiped as idols, or with any other god.
- Witchcraft and the occult. This includes astrology, tarot-card reading, water dousing and any other form of divination.
- Secret Societies. These include Freemasonry and many others. You can add this line to your prayer:

I now renounce the oaths taken by my family members during their involvement with such societies.

- Anti-Semitism and racism.
- Witchcraft done through wrong prayers by Christians— the placing of word curses.
- Sexual sin of any form. This includes homosexuality, bestiality, fornication and adultery.

After praying the prayer, it is time to break the curses that might have come upon you or your family. Pray this prayer out loud with me.

Father, in the name of Jesus Christ of Nazareth, I now break
the following curses off me and my family:
the curse of infirmity
the curse of poverty
the curse of illegitimacy (if appropriate)
the curse of insanity

(Note: If you feel comfortable at this point doing some self-deliverance, read the next section out loud with faith. If possible, have someone you trust help you pray.)

> *I now release myself from all demonic attachments that may*
> *have come through any of the above involvement in those things*
> *that bring the curses. I forbid these spirits from manifesting, in*
> *Jesus' name, or harming me or my loved ones in any way.*
> *In the name of Jesus Christ I now tell the following spirits*
> *to release me:*
> *Spirit of lust and all sexual spirits—release me now in*
> *the name of Jesus*
> *Spirit of infirmity—release me now in the name of Jesus*
> *Spirit of insanity—release me now in the name of Jesus*
> *Spirit of poverty—release me now in the name of Jesus.*

Be open to the leading of the Holy Spirit as to any other demonic powers that you need to dismiss. Check the list that you made of demonic powers you might need to be set free from—now is the time to tell them that they must leave. Call out their names one by one.

(Note: If you suspect that you might be past the beginning stages of demonization, I suggest that you follow the next steps with the direction of a deliverance minister.)

This is also the time when you should renounce and dismiss all spirit guides and family spirits.

> *Father God, in the name of Jesus Christ of Nazareth, I now*
> *command all spirit guides* (give the names if you know
> them) *to leave me now. I also tell all family spirits to leave.*
> *We no longer need you in our family, in Jesus' name!*

If you believe that you have been cursed with a death curse, pray this prayer:

In the Name of Jesus Christ of Nazareth, I now break the spirit of death and all curses of death sent against me. You spirit of death (suicide, death-wish—a spirit that makes you wish you would die), *I command you to leave me now.*

(Note: There are times when fasting is needed to break a curse of death.)

You can pray a similar prayer for any curse that you suspect has been sent against you. There are those who send the curses back against those who are cursing them, and there have been reported cases of occultists throwing up and getting sick. One thing is for sure, it should be known in the heavenly realm that these spirits do not dare touch a child of the living God!

Here is a sample prayer that you can say to break any kind of curse:

I break the (name the kind of curses—word curses, accidents, etc.) *sent against me, in the name of Jesus Christ of Nazareth. Father, I choose to forgive those who have trespassed against me.*

Congratulations! You now have appropriated one of the most precious gifts of your salvation—freedom in Christ! The Word of God gives you this promise:

And you shall know the truth, and the truth shall make you free (John 8:32).

Notes
1. Derek Prince *Blessings or Curse* (Grand Rapids, MI: Chosen Books, 1990), p. 43.
2. Ibid.
3. Cindy Jacobs, *The Voice of God* (Ventura, CA: Regal Books 1995), p. 64.

4. In appendix 1 of this book, I have included a prayer of renunciation from all the curses of freemasonry. I am indebted to Jubilee Ministries for this information.

EPILOGUE

I am aware that some of the material in this book may have made you uncomfortable or even shocked you. One truth that we all need to come back to again and again in our lives as believers is that we are not to fear anything that Satan would try to do to us. We are to be as bold as lions. God has given us authority over all the wiles, methods and schemes of the evil one. We have protection in the name of Jesus Christ. This is true even if we live in a Muslim nation and face overt persecution. And it is true if we live in a land threatened by an occult invasion. As we take up the whole armor of God, we are able to stand against all evil (see Eph. 6:10-13).

Many people have asked me, "Cindy, how have you been able to delve into a study of the occult to the degree that you have and not be afraid?"

My answer is simple: Because I know that greater is He who is in me than He who is in the world (see 1 John 4:4). When I experience difficult times there is an assurance in my heart that if I resist the attack in the name of Jesus, then Satan has to flee and cease and desist! (see Jas. 4:7).

We have been affected by movies and television shows that have shown Satan as being greater than God. Horror movies seem to glorify the power of evil over good. However, for us as believers, nothing could be further from the truth! There is no name greater than His name and no power greater than His power!

Do not let Satan intimidate you and make you afraid of the occult practices and demonic realm that I have uncovered in this book! There is a wonderful promise in 2 Timothy 1:7:

> For God has not given us a spirit of fear, but of power and of love and of a sound mind.

The battleground for most of us is in our minds. If you experienced any kind of fear as you read sections of this book, take time to read the Scriptures on the authority of the believer, which I have included in this epilogue. God wants to take us all to a higher level of authority and to victory in Christ Jesus.

Here is a wonderful promise from Scripture:

> For though we walk in the flesh, we do not war according to the flesh. For the weapons of our warfare are not carnal but mighty in God for pulling down strongholds (2 Cor. 10:10).

With this passage in our hearts, I want to encourage you not to be afraid to speak up if you find that Wiccan teaching is taking place in your child's classroom. A leader in a prayer network that I am familiar with took a stand against the mix of paganism and New Age philosophy being taught at her child's school. She went to the principal to protest and filed a complaint. The teaching was so blatant that the teacher was dismissed from the classroom.

Do not hesitate to visit your child's school library to see if any occult books are on the shelves. If you find any, you have a right to kindly tell school administrators that the material is objectionable and that you would like it removed. If you do not see any action, take the matter to the school board and gather signatures on a petition. One of the reasons that so much occult material has crept into our schools is that many of us have been asleep at the wheel.

A very powerful weapon against the occult invasion in our society is letter writing. Television networks are very much influenced by public opinion. If you see an objectionable show on a certain network, write a letter and object to the content. Even one letter can kick up quite a bit of dust. Write to the mayor, school-board members and local newspapers. Remember the influence one woman named Madalyn Murray O'Hair had on our society? She was the driving force behind prayer being taken out of American public schools in 1962.

I believe that God is raising up men and women of God who are not afraid to stand up and protect our society against the occult influences we see today! We are not out to persecute the Wiccans or any others in the occult. We love those who are Wiccans and do not want any harm to come to them. However, we also know that what they teach does not please God.

While I am encouraging you as believers to effectively protest the occult influences around you, I am also keenly aware that anyone in Wicca may be greatly distressed to read the words I have written. I know that there are some in Wicca who have already been hurt by Christians, as I pointed out in chapter 5. While recognizing this fact, I also realize that many Wiccans are seekers of truth.

If you are one of those Wiccans who is open-minded, would you be willing to try something? Would you pray and ask God if He is really the only true God? Be willing to give God an opportunity to show you that He loves you. You are special to Him, and He would love to prove to you that He is real, is loving and is not the kind of God that those who were Christians in name only made you think He is.

Christians, the last word is for us. We must intercede. We must stand our ground against Satan and the occult. But as we do this, we must remember that God loves every Wiccan, every soothsayer, everyone who has ever read a horoscope, everyone who has played Dungeons and Dragons and anyone who has dabbled in any aspect of the occult. Let's pray for them and be ready to extend open arms to them when they do come to seek the truth of the one true God.

FREEMASONRY
PRAYER

If you or a member of your family has ever been involved with freemasonry, I strongly recommend you say a prayer to break the occult bonds. You can use the following prayer as a model. It is excerpted from *Jubilee Resources* of New Zealand and used by permission. If you or your family were involved with freemasonry at a deep level, I suggest you visit http://www.jubilee.org.nz/free masonry.htm on the Internet. Jubilee Ministries provides prayer guidelines through each level of freemasonry activity.

Father God, creator of heaven and Earth, I come to You in the name of Jesus Christ, Your Son. I come as a sinner seeking forgiveness and cleansing from all sins committed against You, and others made in Your image. I honor my earthly father and mother and all of my ancestors of flesh and blood, and of the spirit by adoption and godparents, but I utterly turn away from and renounce all their sins. I forgive all of my ancestors for the effects of their sins on me and my children. I confess and renounce all of my own sins. I renounce and rebuke Satan and every spiritual power of his affecting me and my family.

I renounce and forsake all involvement in freemasonry or any other lodge or craft by my ancestors and myself. In the name of Jesus Christ, I renounce and cut off witchcraft, the principal spirit behind freemasonry, and I renounce and cut off Baphomet,

*the spirit of antichrist and the spirits of death, and deception. I
renounce the insecurity, the love of position and power, the love
of money, avarice or greed, and the pride which would have led
my ancestors into freemasonry. I renounce all the fears which
held them in freemasonry, especially the fears of death, fears of
men and fears of trusting in the name of Jesus Christ.
I renounce every position held in the lodge by any of my ancestors or myself, including Master, Worshipful Master or any
other. I renounce the calling of any man master, for Jesus
Christ is my only master and Lord, and He forbids anyone else
having that title. I renounce the entrapping of others into
freemasonry, and observing the helplessness of others during the
rituals. I renounce the effects of freemasonry passed on to me
through any female ancestor who felt distrusted and rejected by
her husband as he entered and attended any lodge and refused
to tell her of his secret activities. I also renounce all obligations,
oaths and curses enacted by every female member of my family
through any direct membership of all women's orders of
freemasonry, the Order of the Eastern Star or any other
Masonic or occult organization. . . .
I renounce the all-seeing third eye of freemasonry or Horus in the
forehead and its pagan and occult symbolism. I now close that
third eye and all occult ability to see into the spiritual realm, in
the name of the Lord Jesus Christ, and put my trust in the Holy
Spirit sent by Jesus Christ for all I need to know on spiritual mat-
ters. I renounce all false communions taken, all mockery of the
redemptive work of Jesus Christ on the cross of Calvary, all unbelief, confusion and depression. I renounce and forsake the lie of
freemasonry that man is not sinful, but merely imperfect, and so
can redeem himself through good works. I rejoice that the Bible
states that I cannot do a single thing to earn my salvation, but
that I can only be saved by grace through faith in Jesus Christ and
what He accomplished on the cross of Calvary. . . .*

I renounce all fear of insanity, anguish, death wishes, suicide and death in the name of Jesus Christ. Death was conquered by Jesus Christ and He alone holds the keys of death and hell, and I rejoice that He holds my life in His hands now. He came to give me life abundantly and eternally, and I believe His promises. I renounce all anger, hatred, murderous thoughts, revenge, retaliation, spiritual apathy, false religion, all unbelief, especially unbelief in the Holy Bible as God's Word, and all compromise of God's Word. I renounce all spiritual searching into false religions, and all striving to please God. I rest in the knowledge that I have found my Lord and Savior Jesus Christ, and that He has found me. . . .

I renounce all the other oaths taken, the rituals of every other degree and the curses involved. These include the Allied Degrees, the Red Cross of Constantine, the Order of the Secret Monitor, and the Masonic Royal Order of Scotland. I renounce all other lodges and secret societies including Prince Hall Freemasonry, Grand Orient Lodges, Mormonism, the Order of Amaranth, the Royal Order of Jesters, the Manchester Unity Order of Oddfellows, Buffalos, Druids, Foresters, the Orange and Black Lodges, Elks, Moose and Eagles Lodges, the Ku Klux Klan, the Grange, the Woodmen of the World, Riders of the Red Robe, the Knights of Pythias, the Mystic Order of the Veiled, Prophets of the Enchanted Realm, the women's Orders of the Eastern Star, of the Ladies Oriental Shrine, and of the White Shrine of Jerusalem, the girls' order of the Daughters of the Eastern Star, the International Orders of Job's Daughters, and of the Rainbow, and the boys' Order of De Molay, and their effects on me and all my family. . . .

I renounce every evil spirit associated with masonry and witch-craft and all other sins, and I command in the name of Jesus Christ for Satan and every evil spirit to be bound and to leave me now, touching or harming no one, and go to the place appointed for you by the Lord Jesus, never to return to me or my family. I call on the name of the Lord Jesus to be delivered of these spirits, in accordance with the many promises of the Bible. I ask to be delivered of every spirit of sickness, infirmity, curse, affliction, addiction, disease or allergy associated with these sins I have confessed and renounced. I surrender to God's Holy Spirit and to no other spirit all the places in my life where these sins have been. . . .

I ask You, Lord, to baptize me in Your Holy Spirit now according to the promises in Your Word. I take to myself the whole armor of God in accordance with Ephesians 6, and rejoice in its protection as Jesus surrounds me and fills me with His Holy Spirit. I enthrone You, Lord Jesus, in my heart, for You are my Lord and my Savior, the source of eternal life. Thank You, Father God, for Your mercy, Your forgiveness and Your love, in the name of Jesus Christ, Amen.

TEN STEPS TO RIDDING YOUR HOME OF SPIRITUAL DARKNESS

Step one: Accept Jesus as Your Lord and Savior.

Step two: Take a spiritual inventory of your life.

Step three: Dedicate your home to the Lord.

Step four: Prepare for battle.

Step five: Take a spiritual inventory of your home. Review list of problem objects:

1. foreign gods
2. false religions
3. occult objects
4. secret-society objects and
5. other objects.

Step six :   Cleanse your home of ungodly objects.

Step seven: Cleanse each room and cleanse the land.

Step eight, part 1:   Consecrate your home.

Step eight, part 2:   Consecrate your property.

Step nine: Fill your home with glory.

Step ten: Maintain spiritual victory.

This information is taken from Chuck Pierce's and Rebecca Wagner Sytsema's book *Ridding Your Home of Spiritual Darkness*, published by Wagner Institute for Practical Ministry, P.O. Box 62958, Colorado Springs, CO 80962-2958. Copyright 1999. Used by permission.

OCCULT SIGNS

Anarchy
A symbol that declares the denial of authority.

Ankh
This ancient Egyptian symbol for life has magical implications. The top portion represents the female and the lower half represents the male.

Baphomet
An upside-down pentagram, the two upward points symbolize the devil's horns. The three downward points declare a denial of the trinity. Satan's spirits are supposedly invoked by the downward position of the center point.

Blood Ritual Symbol
The crescent moon is combined with arrows to symbolize human and animal sacrifice.

Church of Satan
The official emblem of the Church of Satan. This depiction has been altered slightly, but it provides an idea of what the mark looks like.

Crescent Moon and Stars

This emblem combines the moon of the goddess Diana and the star, or Lucifer. Such imagery is used in both white and black magic.

Hexagram, or Seal of Solomon

This six-pointed figure resembles the Star of David, but it is not at all the same. The Jewish star represents God's chosen people and His promises to them. When a circle is added around the perimeter, it is corrupted and becomes a powerful occult marker.

Horned Hand

A satanic salute, this portrays the devil's horns. Sometimes it is unknowingly used by people who listen to heavy metal music.

Lightning Bolt

The dramatic presentation of the lightning bolt can represent the *s* in "Satan" or "satanist."

Mark of the Beast

The numbers 666 in various configurations represent the antichrist. This three-circle symbol, while having nonoccult uses, is also used to represent the mark of the beast. This is sometimes written "fff" because *f* is the sixth letter of the alphabet.

Peace Sign

This came to characterize the ideal of peace in the hippie era. But occultists equate the emblem with the cross of Nero. It is meant to depict an inverted and broken Cross and to send out a call to defeat Christianity.

Pentagram, or Pentacle

The top point represents the spirit and the other four points represent wind, fire, earth and water. This emblem is used in both white and black magic.

Sexual Ritual Symbol

A symbol carved into stone or painted along the side of a road to mark the use of the location for a sexual ritual.

Sword of Power

A Celtic weapon often linked with sorcery and fantasy. In Arthurian legend, it was King Arthur's sword of power, or Excalibur, that was thrust into a stone as a test. Arthur and his father, Uther Pendragon, consulted with the sorcerer Merlin, the Celtic sky deity and a British bard.

Upside-Down Cross

A universal mark that connotes rebellion and the denial of Christianity.

Yin/Yang

In Chinese cosmology, yin is female and yang is male. The combination of the two produces all of existence. It can also represent the opposites of day and night, good and evil, and black and white.

GLOSSARY

amulet: A type of protective occult spell worn on an object, such as jewelry, to empower an individual. An object that hangs down off a garment, can be an amulet also. A charm also is a form of amulet when it has a spell spoken over it.

astrology: The study of the stars to foretell the future. This also could include the study of meteors or meteorology.

black magic: Magic done with the intent of harming a person or destroying property.

conjuring or casting spells: Done through the use of herbs, the use of particular words and sacrificing animals or humans. Wiccans use spells to call on the goddesses and gods for their needs, including healing.

coven: A group of Wiccans who meet in secret, usually once a month at the full moon.

divination: To foretell the future through occult means. This is usually done through the use of a familiar spirit or spirit guide. Divination is often done through observing omens like the liver of an animal or a human, tea leaves, tarot cards, crystal balls or other occult apparatus.

enchantment: Another word for magic.

familiar spirit: Used by a soothsayer or fortune-teller to contact a deceased person. This spirit is actually a demon. The term also refers to spirits that attach themselves to families for generations. They demomize the family line and have extensive information on the family.

fortune-telling: An attempt to contact spirits of the dead or of gods to obtain personal insights and direction for the future. God forbids the use of fortune-tellers.

intercession: The act of making a request to a superior or expressing a deep-seated yearning to our one and only superior, God.

magic: a form of communication involving the supernatural world in which an attempt is made to affect the course of present and/or future events by means of ritual action, especially one which involves the symbolic imitation of what the practitioner wants to happen. (This would be the counterfeit for prophetic acts.) Magic also uses formulaic recitations that describe the desired outcome and/or invoke gods, demons or the spirits believed to be resident in natural substances. Magic is an instrument for control.

medium: People who allow familiar spirits or spirit guides to inhabit them to contact the dead and/or to foretell the future.

occult: The word means "hidden." In a negative sense it can be defined as any unbiblical spiritual practice that is inspired or controlled by Satan.

spiritual warfare: The confrontation of the kingdom of darkness by the power of the kingdom of God in order to displace the works of darkness and elevate His Son, Jesus.

Glossary

white magic: Magic done without an evil intent.

Wicca: The modern-day practice of witchcraft. The word means "to bend."

witch: Either a male or female who practices witchcraft, or Wicca.

witchcraft: The practice of dealing with evil spirits. Sorcery is another word for witchcraft. (Wiccans have a different definition because they do not believe they deal with evil spirits.)

Note: Some definitions in this glossary were taken from *Exodus Cry* by Jim W. Goll (Ventura, CA: Regal Books, 2001).

RECOMMENDED READING

Anderson, Neil T. *The Bondage Breaker*. Eugene, OR: Harvest House, 1990.
—— *Spiritual Protection for Your Children*. Ventura, CA: Regal Books, 1996.
Campbell, Ron G. *Free from Freemasonry*. Ventura, CA: Regal Books, 1999.
Gasson, Raphael. *The Challenging Counterfeit*. Gainesville, FL: Bridge-Logos Publishing 1985.
Gibson, Noel and Phyl. *Deliver Our Children from the Evil One*. Tonbridge, Kent, England: Sovereign World, 2000.
—— *Evicting Demonic Intruders*. Tonbridge, Kent, England: Sovereign World, 2000.
Godwin, Rick. *Witchcraft in the Church*. Lake Mary, FL: Creation House, 1997.
Hammond, Frank and Ida Mae. *Pigs in the Parlour: A Practical Guide to Deliverance*. England: New Wine Press, 1990.
Horobin, Peter. *Healing Through Deliverance*. Tonbridge, Kent, England: Sovereign World, 1994.
Jacobs, Cindy. *Possessing the Gates of the Enemy*. Grand Rapids, MI: Chosen Books, 1991.
Koch, Kurt. *Demonology, Past and Present*. Grand Rapids, MI: Kregel Publications, 2000.
Larson, Bob. *Extreme Evil*. Nashville, TN: Thomas Nelson Publishers, 1999.
—— *In the Name of Satan*. Nashville, TN: Thomas Nelson Publishers, 1996.
Lindsay, Gordon. *The Origin of Demons and Their Order*. Dallas, TX: Christ for the Nations Publishing.
Michaelsen, Johanna. *The Beautiful Side of Evil*. Eugene, OR: Harvest House, 1982.
—— *Like Lambs to the Slaughter*. Eugene, OR: Harvest House, 1989.
Pierce, Chuck, and Sytsema, Rebecca. *Ridding Your Home of Spiritual Darkness*. Colorado Springs, CO: Wagner Publishing, 1999.
Prince, Derek. *Blessing or Curse*. Grand Rapids, MI: Chosen Books, 1990.
Robeson, Carol and Jerry. *Strongman's His Name . . . What's His Game?* Wichita, KS: Shiloh Publishing House, 1987.
Sandford, John and Mark. *Deliverance and Inner Healing*. Grand Rapids, MI: Chosen Books, 1992.
Schnoebelen, William. *Satan's Little White Lie*. Chino, CA: Chick Publications, 1990.

Sherrer, Quin, and Garlock, Ruthanne. *A Woman's Guide to Spiritual Warfare*. Ann Arbor, MI: Vine Books, 1991.

Stokes, Burton, and Lucas, Lynn. *No Longer a Victim*. Shippensburg, PA: Destiny Image Publishers, 1995.

Sumrall, Lester. *Demons: The Answer Book*. Nashville, TN: Thomas Nelson Publishers, 1979.

Wagner, Doris M. *How to Cast Out Demons: A Guide to the Basics*. Ventura, CA: Regal Books, 2000.

INDEX

Generals★org
Getting The Word Out!

Visit our website and learn more about the ministry of Cindy Jacobs at www.generals.org.

Cindy Jacobs

Other books / series by Cindy Jacobs:

Possessing The Gates of the Enemy (Baker Books)

The Voice of God (Gospel Light)

Women of Destiny (Gospel Light)

Righteous Revolution (Audio series)

Deliverance From Evil (Audio series)

Women of Destiny (Audio and Video series)

Possessing the Gates of the Enemy (Video series)

For more information about Cindy Jacobs,

call : (719)535-0977 fax : (719)535-0884

email : generals@generals.org

Or mail to : 1035 Garden of the Gods Rd.

Colorado Springs, CO 80907